Learning Trajectories for Teachers

Learning Trajectories for Teachers

Designing Effective Professional Development for Math Instruction

EDITED BY
Paola Sztajn
P. Holt Wilson

TEACHERS COLLEGE PRESS
TEACHERS COLLEGE | COLUMBIA UNIVERSITY
NEW YORK AND LONDON

NATIONAL COUNCIL OF
TEACHERS OF MATHEMATICS

Published simultaneously by Teachers College Press, 1234 Amsterdam Avenue, New York, NY 10027 and by NCTM, 1906 Association Drive, Reston, VA 20191-1502.

Cover images: Rainbow courtesy of Silver Blu3 via a creative commons attribution license; math notations by nzphotonz / iStock by Getty Images.

Library of Congress Cataloging-in-Publication Data

Names: Sztajn, Paola, 1964- editor. | Wilson, P. Holt (Peter Holt)
Title: Learning trajectories for teachers : designing effective professional development for math instruction / edited by Paola Sztajn, P. Holt Wilson.
Description: New York, NY : Teachers College Press, [2019] | Includes bibliographical references and index. |
Identifiers: LCCN 2019002942 (print) | LCCN 2019010544 (ebook) |
ISBN 9780807777817 (ebook)
ISBN 9780807761441 (pbk. : alk. paper)
Subjects: LCSH: Mathematics teachers—In-service training. | Mathematics teachers—Training of. | Curriculum planning.
Classification: LCC QA10.5 (ebook) | LCC QA10.5 .L43285 2019 (print) | DDC 372.7/044—dc23
LC record available at https://lccn.loc.gov/2019002942

ISBN 978-0-8077-6144-1 (paper)
ISBN 978-0-8077-6179-3 (hardcover)
ISBN 978-0-8077-7781-7 (ebook)

Printed on acid-free paper
Manufactured in the United States of America

Contents

Acknowledgments

Putting an edited volume together requires the work of many. We owe a great debt to all who agreed to partner with us in this journey and who made this book possible. We are thankful to Sarah Biondello, Joy Mizan, Dan Rick-creek, Jennifer Baker, and their colleagues at Teachers College Press for supporting and believing in this project. Our most sincere appreciation also goes to the contributing authors in this book for their partnership and engagement with the process. From when we first started discussing the potential of bringing our projects together in one volume to the actual completion of the manuscript, our colleagues have enlightened us with key insights and indulged us with their patience and willingness to participate in this work. Thanks are also due to our families for their unwavering patience in allowing us time to work on this project. We also want to acknowledge the National Science Foundation for funding the work of all projects represented in this book and for supporting the meeting that first brought contributing authors together to discuss similarities and differences across our professional development projects. This initial meeting led us to envision the possibilities for this book. Finally, to the teachers who participated in the professional development projects discussed herein, our most sincere thank you. Without you, there would be no book or reason to work on one! You are the main contributors to our learning.

CHAPTER 1

Learning Trajectories and Professional Development

Paola Sztajn and P. Holt Wilson

When Ms. Williams, an elementary school teacher, is teaching her mathematics lessons, she knows her goals for every task she uses. She knows the *content* of the lesson and understands how this particular lesson fits within her mathematics objectives for the unit. She uses this knowledge to decide on probing questions to pose to her students as they work on the tasks and later discuss their work. Ms. Williams also knows her *students* and understands how students at different places in their learning engage with the tasks at hand. When planning her lesson, Ms. Williams anticipates what different students might need and prepares for a few different instructional scenarios, so that during the lesson she can be ready to work with students who need scaffolding to get started, as well as with others who need further challenges to remain engaged. As students work on the tasks, Ms. Williams pays attention to more and less mathematically advanced ways in which students approach tasks and supports each and every student in deepening their understanding of the topic. She then asks a few students to share their work with the whole group to engage the class in productive mathematics discussions. Ms. Williams considers the mistakes students are making, what these mistakes reveal about students' understanding of the topic, and how she will work with them as the lesson continues to unfold. She assigns follow-up tasks to different groups of students, and, for each of these groups, Ms. Williams has a solid understanding of what she wants them to learn next.

This portrait of Ms. Williams shows an elementary school teacher with a framework of student thinking at the center of her instruction. She uses this framework to interpret what students know and are yet to know and to guide her teaching, from task selection to student engagement to assessment. There was a time when Ms. Williams' hard work to understand the mathematics she teaches and develop the depth of her content knowledge (characterized in the first few sentences of the portrait) was enough to warrant what was considered good instruction. Though it is still the case that strong knowledge of the content is a requirement for good instruction, we now know that content knowledge alone does not suffice! With a growing understanding about how students informally think about mathematics and develop mathematical ideas over time, great teachers like Ms. Williams seek out and use new knowledge about student learning (characterized in the remainder of the portrait). Good instruction rests upon knowledge of learners together with knowledge of content. Thus, excellent teachers know how their students learn, and use frameworks to organize this knowledge in ways that help them think about their teaching. These frameworks are often called learning trajectories (LTs). When teachers use them to make decisions about their teaching, as Ms. Williams does, they are engaged in what we call *learning trajectory based instruction* (Sztajn, Confrey, Wilson, & Edgington, 2012).

This book is about supporting teachers to strengthen their teaching, in keeping with our sketch of the teacher we describe as Ms. Williams. It focuses on understanding how teachers can learn to make LTs central to their teaching, engaging in learning trajectory based instruction. More specifically, the book shares the stories of four different professional development projects designed to promote teacher learning and the use of frameworks of student thinking—a research tool of growing interest to professional development designers (Sztajn, Borko, & Smith, 2017). The book represents an effort to look across projects that promote teacher learning of learning trajectory based instruction and discuss what these projects reveal about the design of such professional development (PD). It aims to inform professional development designers and teacher educators who want to improve their work in promoting teacher learning of LTs. It is also useful for teachers who want to use LTs to support their students' learning as well as for researchers interested in teacher education or PD. We begin with a brief introduction to LTs before discussing PD centered on these trajectories.

WHAT ARE LEARNING TRAJECTORIES?

Analyzing his own teaching of mathematics, Simon (1995) captured the interest of mathematics education researchers when he coined the concept of a hypothetical learning trajectory. He suggested that mathematics instruction starts with a learning goal for the students, a hypothesis about what students currently understand and how their understanding evolves, and a set of learning activities to support students along that path. Together, the goal, the learning hypothesis, and the activities made up what, at the time, Simon (1995) called a hypothetical learning trajectory. In his words:

> The teacher's learning goal provides a direction for a hypothetical learning trajectory. I use the term "hypothetical learning trajectory" to refer to the teacher's prediction as to the path by which learning might proceed. It is hypothetical because the actual learning

trajectory is not knowable in advance . . . A hypothetical learning trajectory provides the teacher with a rationale for choosing a particular instructional design; thus, I make my design decisions based on my best guess on how learning might proceed.

The choice of the word "trajectory" is meant to refer to a path, the nature of which can perhaps be clarified by the following analogy. Consider that you have decided to sail around the world in order to visit places that you have never seen. . . . You may initially plan the whole trip or only part of it. You set out sailing according to your plan. However, you must constantly adjust because of the conditions that you encounter. . . . You change your plans with respect to the order of your destination. You modify the length and nature of your visits as a result of your interactions with people along the way. You add destinations that prior to your trip were unknown to you. The path that you travel is your "trajectory." The path that you anticipate at any point in time is your "hypothetical trajectory." (p. 136)

The idea that teachers construct these hypothetical trajectories was profound. It spoke to teachers' agency in the classroom as they engage with students and work to understand their thinking. It also showed that effective teachers do not approach a learning situation without knowledge about their students and an initial plan for students' learning. This plan unfolds and changes into actualized learning through interactions with the students, building on and reorganizing the teachers' initial predictions and the activities and goals that go with them.

Following Simon's initial work, a new question arose: What if we substituted teachers' best guesses for shared knowledge? The idea was that instead of teachers making instructional decisions "based on [their] best guess on how learning might proceed" (p. 136) they could make decisions based on shared knowledge about how learning might proceed. Teachers' instructional decisions could be based on research on learning that is organized into trajectories, and these trajectories would be empirically developed and tested to give teachers a tool that represents how students' learning might proceed in a particular topic. This tool would then be used in several classrooms with many students, year after year. The trajectories would still be hypothetical, as in Simon's explanation of the sailing trip, functioning as starting points for teachers to work with students during instruction. However, teachers would not be recreating these trajectories alone or every time; instead they would use shared, research-based trajectories in the implementation and discussions of instructional decisions. This was an intriguing idea.

The concept of empirically developed, shared trajectories that mapped student learning captivated the imagination of educational researchers. Such trajectories could serve as a tool to guide curriculum development or provide a foundation for assessments to diagnose and monitor student learning. For teachers, trajectories could assist them in understanding their students' thinking and provide a framework to guide their actions in planning, implementing, and reflecting on a lesson. Over time, the possibility of such a shared path for student learning coalesced into the current attention to the concept of LTs and learning trajectory based instruction.

The concept of evidence-based mappings of students' learning, however, was not new. In their seminal work in the 1980s, Carpenter and Moser (1984) had created a framework of student thinking about addition and subtraction problems that later led to the work on Cognitively Guided Instruction (CGI) (Carpenter, Fennema, Franke, Levi, & Empson, 2015). This pioneering effort provided the foundation for teachers to use knowledge about the development of student thinking to inform their practice and, to date, Cognitively Guided Instruction remains one of the few approaches to teacher professional development that has demonstrated positive impacts on student learning (Wilson & Berne, 1999). Simon's work, nonetheless, brought forth the powerful idea of instruction that is guided by LTs, which, about 10 years later, emerged in a wave of attention to the topic.

By 2007, a National Research Council committee attending to the learning and teaching of science in schools released a report that called on researchers who examined student learning to map such learning into trajectories[1] that "describe the successively more sophisticated ways of thinking about a topic that can follow and build on one another as children learn about and investigate a topic over a broad span of time (e.g., 6 to 8 years)" (National Research Council, 2007, p. 213). The committee underscored that trajectories were "a promising direction" for organizing instruction and suggested that further research and development was needed to create these frameworks to support students' understanding. The National Research Council book was a catalyst to already existing interest among researchers about the idea of LTs (e.g., Battista, 2004; Clements & Sarama, 2004; Shapiro, 2004), and several conferences, publications, and policy briefs followed.

In addition to the broad definition used by the National Research Council, other definitions have been proposed for LTs. For example, Clements and Sarama (2004) defined LTs as "descriptions of children's thinking and learning in a specific mathematical domain, and a related conjectured route through a set of instructional tasks designed to engender those mental processes or actions hypothesized to move children through a developmental progression of levels of thinking" (p. 83). Confrey, Maloney, Nguyen, Mojica, and Myers (2009) defined a LT as "a researcher-conjectured, empirically-supported description of the ordered network of constructs a student encounters through instruction (i.e., activities, tasks, tools, forms of interaction, and methods of evaluation), in order to move from informal ideas, through successive refinements of representation, articulation, and reflection, towards increasingly complex concepts over time" (p. 347).

These definitions and others suggest variations in the object of learning, scale, and theoretical perspective considered in different LTs (Lobato & Walters, 2017). Yet these definitions also point to the idea that LTs provide an initial mapping of student learning that can guide teachers' instructional decisions and exist in the context of teacher/learner interactions, when trajectories become "real" through instruction.

USING LEARNING TRAJECTORIES IN INSTRUCTION

The potential of LTs in supporting instruction was recognized by the greater education community when researchers called for translating them into "usable tools for teachers" (Daro, Mosher, & Corcoran, 2011, p. 13). Still, much of the initial work on the use of LTs in mathematics education focused on policy (e.g., Common Core; Corcoran, Mosher, & Rogat, 2009), assessment (e.g., Battista, 2004; Gotwals & Songer, 2013; Confrey & Maloney, 2012), curriculum development (Clements, 2007), or the connections among them (e.g., Confrey, Maloney, & Corley, 2014; Daro, Mosher, & Corcoran, 2011; Duncan & Hmelo-Silver, 2009). This initial work was similar in science education, where Shapiro (2004) introduced the idea of learning progressions to offer curriculum developers insights into how students learn over long periods of time and how this learning is organized. As in mathematics education, most of this work was focused on the research and development of tools for teaching—and not on the actual teaching of mathematics or science.

How teachers interpret and use LTs as instructional tools is a much more recent object of research attention (Lobato & Walters, 2017). The authors of chapters in this book have made significant contributions to this line of research, and their efforts have provided insights about how teachers come to learn and use LTs in their classrooms. The paragraphs below highlight some of these insights.

Researchers in the Learning Trajectory Based Instruction project (Chapter 2) have shown that teachers can use LTs to select tasks and interact with students (Wilson, 2009), addressing students' misconceptions (Edgington, 2012). Teachers' own content knowledge, however, matters when they interact with and learn about the trajectories (Wilson, Sztajn, Edgington, & Confrey, 2014). In the classroom, teachers can use LTs to anticipate students' strategies, monitor small-group work, and sequence large-group discussions (Wilson, Sztajn, Edgington, & Myers, 2015). Teachers can also use LTs to learn to talk differently about their students. LTs, nonetheless, do not challenge existing talk that includes deficit language about mathematical abilities (Wilson, Sztajn, Edgington, Webb, & Myers, 2017).

Researchers in the Children's Measurement Project (Chapter 3) have found that LTs can support teachers' focus on the conceptual building blocks of mathematical content (Wickstrom, Baek, Barrett, Tobias, & Cullen, 2012). Teachers who learn about trajectories can develop more specific language and lesson designs. They can also use the levels in the trajectories to mark students' partial progress instead of expecting an "all or nothing" understanding (Wickstrom, 2014). Teachers benefit from LTs as prompts to explore conceptual aspects of mathematical content, building their own content knowledge for teaching (e.g, Wickstrom & Jurczak, 2016; Wickstrom, Nelson, & Chumbley, 2015).

Focusing on instructional practices that build on students' thinking, researchers in the Responsive Teaching in Elementary Mathematics Project (Chapter 4) have revealed the critical role of noticing a student's mathematical thinking (Jacobs, Lamb, & Philipp, 2010). Focusing on teachers' responses, researchers have identified categories of questioning that build on students' thinking (Jacobs & Ambrose, 2008; Jacobs & Empson, 2016). They have highlighted the purpose of each category. These categories are important because questioning that is grounded in the specific details of students' thinking provides increased opportunities for students to advance their understanding (Jacobs, Franke, Carpenter, Levi, & Battey, 2007; Steinberg, Empson, & Carpenter, 2004).

Research in the Building Blocks and TRIAD Projects (Chapter 5) showed that when teachers participate in PD on LTs, their practices improve and there are increases in children's achievement in mathematics and also in other domains, such as language. Teachers demonstrate increasing levels of fidelity in implementing ideas from the professional development on LTs both 2 years and 6 years after the professional development (Sarama, Lange, Clements, & Wolfe, 2012). For these researchers, LTs that include mathematics goals, developmental progression of levels of children's thinking, and instructional tasks and strategies linked to specific levels provide the conditions for promoting sustainability in teacher practices. Research suggests these trajectories can address a climate of low expectations in some urban schools as teachers increase their understanding of the capacities of all children to learn mathematics.

In the chapters that follow, the researchers who contributed to these and other findings discuss what they have learned through their experiences in designing and providing professional development around LTs. More important, they go beyond their research findings to discuss their practice as professional development designers and share their assumptions and experiences in developing and providing these professional development programs. They attend to their work in conceptualizing, creating, leading, or scaling mathematics professional development for elementary school teachers and present lessons learned.

MATHEMATICS TEACHING AND PROFESSIONAL DEVELOPMENT

It is important to consider LTs in the context of what constitutes high-quality instruction. This type of instruction is ambitious in its goal of advancing the mathematical understanding of each and every student (Lampert, Beasley, Ghousseini, Kazemi, & Franke, 2010), not only promoting instruction guided by trajectories but also fostering equitable learning trajectory based instruction (Myers, Sztajn, Wilson, & Edgington, 2015). The vision for mathematics teaching that is key for the design of many professional development programs in mathematics is also central for the programs presented in this book. This vision includes "instruction that builds on rich mathematical tasks, attends to student thinking, values interactions as a learning mechanism, and is considered 'ambitious'" (Sztajn, Borko, & Smith, 2017, p. 796).

Jacobs and Spangler (2017) proposed that this type of teaching attends to student thinking and is contingent on students' comments, questions, and strategies. They highlighted that such teaching benefits teachers and students: "When teachers explore students' ways of reasoning, they benefit by gaining a window into students' reasoning, which can be mathematically powerful but often differs from teachers' reasoning. Students benefit because they not only have opportunities to articulate and reflect on their reasoning but also learn to value their own and peers' sense making" (p. 767).

This vision for high-quality mathematics instruction aligns with the idea of learning trajectory based instruction in which LTs are central and shape teachers' mathematical knowledge for teaching, task selection, orchestration of discourse, formative assessment, and equitable practices. LTs can also be placed at the center of practices considered core for mathematics instruction, such as teacher noticing and leading discussions (Jacobs & Spangler, 2017). Given the central role of instruction in learning, as well as recent progress in better articulating important features of high-quality mathematics instruction and equitable teaching, it is important to continue to articulate the vision for instruction that guides the work of those designing professional development focused on LTs and learning trajectory based instruction.

DESIGN OF PROFESSIONAL DEVELOPMENT

Of particular importance to this book is attention to how to best design programs that address the key ideas about LTs while also attending to what is known about effective professional development. Thus, we want to highlight some shared features across the professional development programs discussed in this book. All programs build on current consensus features of quality professional development, such as implementation over a significant number of hours, spanning many months, having a content focus on mathematics teaching and learning, and using pedagogies that promote teachers' active learning. However, as Sztajn, Borko, and Smith (2017) suggested, the programs understand these features as necessary features of effective professional development but far from sufficient to explain what makes professional development successful. In the accompanying chapters, each of the professional development programs attends to the specific design features of its program. The authors discuss what makes their professional development effective and the ways in which frameworks of student thinking are central to their projects. Perhaps more interesting, they discuss what they learned in the process of designing and implementing their professional development.

When designing learning opportunities for teachers, professional developers attend to teachers' learning goals and interests and to how teachers help shape the design of their own learning. It is also important to consider that teachers learn in the context of their classrooms, within their schools, and in interaction with their colleagues. Thus, practice plays a key role in the design of professional development, and the programs presented make use of important artifacts of practice such as video clips or student work. Understanding how these various tools were used in different programs, and the lessons learned from such use, can improve the use of such tools when designing other professional development programs for student thinking frameworks in different contexts. Those seeking to take ideas from the programs presented here into their own practice can benefit from the detailed descriptions the chapters provide concerning program design, what teachers learned, and what researchers learned.

CAUTION POINTS ABOUT LEARNING TRAJECTORIES

Before discussing how LTs can serve as starting points to guide instruction and the design of professional development, we acknowledge that the research on LTs has not come without criticism and potential pitfalls. We also recognize that skeptical criticism is a fundamental part of the knowledge development process. Thus, in this section we briefly present concerns that have emerged regarding LT research.

An important idea when considering LTs is that researchers' perspectives on learning shape the development of the trajectories. Lobato and Walters (2017) reported that different perspectives on learning have been used in the development of different trajectories. Perspectives that attend to learning as a social, rather than an individual, phenomenon are underrepresented in LT research. This implies that, in many cases, the learning described in LTs is conceived as paths for individuals to gain knowledge, when, for many researchers, learning is not the isolated experience of single individuals. For several of the projects in this book, learning is a social phenomenon, or should at least be considered from a combination of outlooks that includes both the individual and collective views of learning. From a more social perspective on learning, trajectories are negotiated in the larger context of classroom interactions as well as in professional development settings.

The idea of trajectories as paths for individuals to gain knowledge can lead to a problematic interpretation that suggests every student follows the steps specified in LTs as they learn. Empson (2011) showed that, even in topics such as students' strategies for solving addition and subtraction problems, where there is robust evidence for a progression of learning, students' use of these strategies varies between classrooms and children. This means that the development of student learning is highly context-dependent and should not be equated with the following of predetermined steps from a trajectory. It is important to understand that LTs represent common patterns in aspects of learning, rather than a determined path. In her early work, Confrey (2006) suggested that trajectories provide conceptual corridors with landmarks as well as constraints and obstacles. Teachers and students navigate these corridors, finding their paths from prior knowledge to learned ideas.

There are also concerns about equity regarding the research used to generate LTs, particularly about the lack of attention to the variety of cultural practices learners bring to learning situations (Anderson et al., 2012). Myers (2014) problematized the paucity of questions about the reproduction of systems of class, race, and gender in LT research. She suggested that particular attention be given to understanding how cultural artifacts can limit learning opportunities for certain students, particularly students of color. Myers also called for further attention to the students participating in the empirical research used to develop and validate LTs. She suggested that when such research does not attend to the diversity of its sample, it can privilege the knowledge of particular groups in the development of LTs while affirming the resulting trajectories as universal. Myers suggested that we carefully examine the concept of universality in research results such as LTs.

For the authors in this book, attention to potential pitfalls in research on LTs is of utmost importance and needs to guide those supporting teacher learning and use of these trajectories. In particular, equity in mathematics instruction is a central tenet for mathematics education and needs to be at the forefront of research on how teachers come to use LTs in diverse classrooms. Still, the agreement that research can address emerging concerns and work toward the development of shared, empirically tested, continuously improved frameworks about student learning remains key to the work of authors in this book. Further, these frameworks are useful starting points for teachers across contexts and groups of students.

OVERVIEW OF THE BOOK

In October 2016, the researchers working on the four projects presented in this book met to discuss what they were learning from their various projects centered on teacher learning.[2] The goal of the 2-day meeting was to share, accumulate, and synthesize evidence of what teachers learn and how they use frameworks of student thinking across the four projects. Descriptions of what happens inside each professional development and how professional learning tasks are designed to foster teacher learning were at the center of the conversations. The meeting also highlighted similarities and differences across projects. Attention to issues of equity emerged as a fundamental point in the discussion among researchers.

The conversations that took place during the meeting strengthened the collaboration across projects and led to this book. The meeting generated recommendations for professional development focused on LTs—which are embedded throughout the chapters in the book and further highlighted in Chapter 6. Chapters 2–5 are organized around the four projects participating in the meeting.

In Chapter 2, Sztajn, Edgington, Wilson, Webb, and Myers describe the Learning Trajectory Based Instruction project. Attending to the issue of how to bring a research-developed tool such as LTs to teachers in ways that promote productive research and practice connections, they discuss their design of a professional development program that was respectful of teachers' knowledge. For them, professional development is a space in which teachers and researchers come together to share knowledge and learn from each other. Thus, they examine how they adapted LTs—created by researchers—to be useful to teachers. They present the principles they used to create professional learning tasks around these trajectories.

In Chapter 3, Barrett, Wickstrom, Tobias, Cullen, Cullen, and Baek examine the Children's Measurement Project: Sharing Trajectories with Teachers. Here they integrate LT research into their professional development to help teachers look more fcarefully at students' thinking, modify or develop tasks, and use lesson study as a structure to improve the teaching of geometric measurement. Specifically, they want teachers to use the trajectories for formative assessment in the classroom. The authors discuss how the project supported teachers' task design as well as their noticing and responding to students' mathematics.

In Chapter 4, Jacobs, Empson, Pynes, Hewitt, Jessup, and Krause discuss the Responsive Teaching in Elementary Mathematics (RTEM) project. Their focus is on professional development that helps teachers develop instruction that is responsive to children's fraction thinking. Responsive teaching requires expertise in eliciting and attending to the details of children's thinking to make decisions in the midst of instruction. To support teachers in developing this expertise, these authors work with frameworks that encapsulate research on children's thinking and on the instructional practices of noticing children's thinking and questioning to build on children's thinking. They identify design principles that create opportunities for teachers to integrate these frameworks into their teaching.

In Chapter 5, Sarama and Clements examine the design, scale-up, and evaluation of a professional development based on LTs in the context of the Building Blocks and TRIAD projects. With attention to the development of evidence-based curriculum materials and a focus on equity, the chapter shows how these projects built on the 10 phases from Clements's (2007) Curriculum Reform Framework. The authors discuss how they designed a professional development focused on teachers learning to engage young children in mathematics that is both appropriate and challenging, and they touch on the fidelity of teachers' implementation of what they learned. They examine the challenges of designing a program that can be delivered at scale and discuss principles that can support both implementation and sustainability long after the original professional development ends.

All the authors present principles that guided the projects' professional development design, provide rationales for professional development features, describe key decisions that shaped the resulting programs, and share what the designers learned in the process of developing and enacting their professional development. Such attention to design provides a rare opportunity to identify and examine key factors that influence both the implementation of the professional development and teacher learning. Therefore, in Chapter 6, we examine issues regarding professional development design discussed in Chapters 2–5. We present important design features for professional development in general as well as for professional development that focuses on frameworks of student thinking. In particular, we discuss issues related to the ways in which trajectories are presented to teachers as well as connections between trajectories and instruction. We also turn to the issues of context and equity and offer a set of recommendations for designing professional development for LTs. This summary chapter is followed by Chapter 7, in which Hilda Borko adds her perspective on the book. She looks at LTs as conceptual tools for professional development design and connects the ideas in this book to larger discussions on professional development.

NOTES

1. In science education, the term *learning progression* is used more often than *trajectory*. For this book, we use the word *trajectory* instead of *progression* whenever possible, in alignment with the discursive practice and perspective of the mathematics education community.

2. This report is based on a meeting supported by the National Science Foundation grant DRL-1008364. Any opinions, findings, and conclusions or recommendations expressed in this report are those of the authors and do not necessarily reflect the views of the foundation.

REFERENCES

Anderson, C. W., Cobb, P., Calabrese Barton, A., Confrey, J., Penuel, W. R., & Schauble, L. (2012). *Learning Progressions Footprint Conference Final Report*. East Lansing, MI: Michigan State University.

Battista, M. T. (2004). Applying cognition-based assessment to elementary school students' development of understanding area and volume measurement. *Mathematical Thinking and Learning, 6*(2), 185–204.

Carpenter, T. P., Fennema, E., Franke, M. L., Levi, L., & Empson, S. B. (2015). *Children's mathematics: Cognitively guided instruction* (2nd ed.). Portsmouth, NH: Heinemann.

Carpenter, T. P., & Moser, J. M. (1984). The acquisition of addition and subtraction concepts in grades one through three. *Journal for Research in Mathematics Education, 15*(3), 179–202.

Clements, D. H. (2007). Curriculum research: Toward a framework for "Research-based curricula." *Journal for Research in Mathematics Education, 38*(1), 35–70.

Clements, D. H., & Sarama, J. (2004). Learning trajectories in mathematics education. *Mathematical Thinking and Learning, 6*, 81–89.

Confrey, J. (2006). The evolution of design studies as methodology. In K. Sawyer (Ed.), *The Cambridge handbook of the learning sciences* (pp. 131–151). New York, NY: Cambridge University Press.

Confrey, J., & Maloney, A. P. (2012). Next-generation digital classroom assessment based on learning trajectories. In C. Dede & J. Richards (Eds.) *Digital teaching platforms: Customizing classroom learning for each student* (pp. 134–152). New York, NY: Teachers College Press.

Confrey, J., Maloney, A. P., & Corley, A. (2014). Learning trajectories: A framework for connecting standards with curriculum. *ZDM Mathematics Education, 46*(5), 719–733.

Confrey, J., Maloney, A. P., Nguyen, K., Mojica, G., & Myers, M. (2009). Equipartitioning/ splitting as a foundation of rational number reasoning using learning trajectories. *Proceedings of the 33rd Conference of the International Group for the Psychology of Mathematics Education*. PME 33, Thessaloniki, Greece.

Corcoran, T., Mosher, F. A., & Rogat, A. (2009). *Learning progressions in science: An evidence-based approach to reform.* Retrieved from https://repository.upenn.edu/cpre_researchreports/53/

Daro, P., Mosher, F. A., & Corcoran, T. (2011). *Learning trajectories in mathematics* (Research Report No. 68). Madison, WI: Consortium for Policy Research in Education.

Duncan, R., & Hmelo-Silver, C. (2009). Learning progressions: Aligning curriculum, instruction, and assessment. *Journal of Research in Science Teaching, 46*(6), 606–609.

Edgington, C. (2012). Teachers' uses of a learning trajectory to support attention to student thinking in the mathematics classroom (Unpublished doctoral dissertation). North Carolina State University, Raleigh, NC.

Empson, S. B. (2011). On the idea of learning trajectories: Promises and pitfalls. *The Mathematics Enthusiast, 8*(3), 571–598.

Gotwals, A. W., & Songer, N. B. (2013). Validity evidence for learning progression-based assessment items that fuse core disciplinary ideas and science practices. *Journal of Research in Science Teaching, 50*(5), 597–626.

Jacobs, V. R., & Ambrose, R. C. (2008). Making the most of story problems. *Teaching Children Mathematics, 15*, 260–266.

Jacobs, V. R., & Empson, S. B. (2016). Responding to children's mathematical thinking in the moment: an emerging framework of teaching moves. *ZDM, 48*(1–2), 185–197.

Jacobs, V. R., Franke, M. L., Carpenter, T. P., Levi, L., & Battey, D. (2007). Professional development focused on children's algebraic reasoning in elementary school. *Journal for Research in Mathematics Education, 38*(3), 258–288.

Jacobs, V. R., Lamb, L. L. C., & Philipp, R. A. (2010). Professional noticing of children's mathematical thinking. *Journal for Research in Mathematics Education, 41*(2), 169–202.

Jacobs, V. R., & Spangler, D. A. (2017). Research on core practices in K–12 mathematics teaching. In J. Cai (Ed.), *Compendium for Research in Mathematics Education*, (pp. 766–792). Reston, VA: National Council of Teachers of Mathematics.

Lampert, M., Beasley, H., Ghousseini, H., Kazemi, E., & Franke, M. L. (2010). Using designed instructional activities to enable novices to manage ambitious mathematics teaching. In M. K. Stein & L. Kucan (Eds.), *Instructional explanations in the disciplines*, (pp. 129–141). New York, NY: Springer.

Lobato, J., & Walters, C. D. (2017) A taxonomy of approaches to learning trajectories and progressions. In J. Cai (Ed.), *Compendium for Research in Mathematics Education*, (pp. 74–101). Reston, VA: National Council of Teachers of Mathematics.

Myers, M. (2014). *The use of learning trajectory based instruction in supporting equitable teaching practices in elementary classrooms: A multi-case study* (Unpublished doctoral dissertation). North Carolina State University, Raleigh, NC.

Myers, M., Sztajn, P., Wilson, P. H., & Edgington, C. (2015). From implicit to explicit: Articulating equitable learning trajectories based instruction. *Journal of Urban Mathematics Education, 8*(2), 11–22.

National Research Council (2007). *Taking science to school.* Washington, DC: National Academy Press.

Sarama, J., Lange, A., Clements, D. H., & Wolfe, C. B. (2012). The impacts of an early mathematics curriculum on emerging literacy and language. *Early Childhood Research Quarterly, 27*(3), 489–502. doi:10.1016/j.ecresq.2011.12.002

Shapiro, B. (2004). Developing understanding: Research on science learning and teaching over time. *Canadian Journal Science, Mathematics, and Technology Education, 4*(1), 1–6.

Simon, M. A. (1995). Reconstructing mathematics pedagogy from a constructivist perspective. *Journal for Research in Mathematics Education, 26*(2), 114–145.

Steinberg, R., Empson, S. B., & Carpenter, T. P. (2004). Inquiry into children's mathematical thinking as a means to teacher change. *Journal of Mathematics Teacher Education, 7*(3), 237–267.

Sztajn, P., Borko, H., & Smith, T. S. (2017). Research on mathematics professional development. In J. Cai (Ed.), *Compendium for Research in Mathematics Education*, (pp. 793–823). Reston, VA: National Council of Teachers of Mathematics.

Sztajn, P., Confrey, J., Wilson, P. H., & Edgington, C. (2012). Learning trajectory based instruction: Toward a theory of teaching. *Educational Researcher, 41*(5), 147–156.

Wickstrom, M. H. (2014). *An examination of teachers' perceptions and implementation of learning trajectory based professional development* (Doctoral dissertation). Illinois State University, Normal, IL.

Wickstrom, M. H., Baek, J. M., Barrett, J. E., Tobias, J., & Cullen, C. J. (2012, November). *Teachers' noticing of children's understanding of linear measurement.* Paper presented at the Proceedings of the 34th annual meeting of the North American

Chapter of the International Group for the Psychology of Mathematics Education, Kalamazoo, MI.

Wickstrom, M. H., & Jurczak, L. M. (2016). Inch by inch, we measure. *Teaching Children Mathematics, 22*(8), 468–475.

Wickstrom, M. H., Nelson, J., & Chumbley, J. (2015). Area conceptions sprout on Earth Day. *Teaching Children Mathematics, 21*(4), 466–474.

Wilson, P. H. (2009). *Teachers' uses of a learning trajectory for equipartitioning* (Unpublished doctoral dissertation). North Carolina State University, Raleigh, NC.

Wilson, P. H., Sztajn, P., Edgington, C., & Confrey, J. (2014). Teachers' use of their mathematical knowledge for teaching in learning a mathematics learning trajectory. *Journal of Mathematics Teacher Education, 17*(2), 149–175.

Wilson, P. H., Sztajn, P., Edgington, C., & Myers, M. (2015). Teachers' uses of a learning trajectory in student-centered instructional practices. *Journal of Teacher Education, 66*(3), 227–244.

Wilson, P. H., Sztajn, P., Edgington, C., Webb, J., & Myers, M. (2017). Change in teachers' discourse about students in a professional development on learning trajectories. *American Educational Research Journal, 54*(3), 568–604.

Wilson, S. M., & Berne, J. (1999). Teacher learning and the acquisition of professional knowledge: An examination of research on contemporary professional development. *Review of Research in Education, 24*(1), 173–209.

CHAPTER 2

The Learning Trajectory Based Instruction Project

Paola Sztajn, Cyndi Edgington, P. Holt Wilson,
Jared Webb, and Marrielle Myers

Before the release of the Common Core State Standards for Mathematics (National Governors Association [NGA] Center for Best Practices and the Council of Chief State School Officers [CCSSO], 2010), most teachers had never heard of learning trajectories (LTs). Education researchers, however, had been working to pull together and order results from studies on student learning to create frameworks that describe how students develop key mathematical concepts over time. These frameworks eventually became known as LTs, and from the very beginning, researchers used them to create tools to support instruction, such as evidence-based curricular materials (e.g., *Building Blocks*; see Chapter 5), or assessments that can assist teachers in determining what students had learned and what they should learn next (Battista, 2004; Confrey & Maloney, 2012). When the Common Core was published, it stated that "the development of the standards began with research-based learning progressions detailing what is known today about how students' mathematical knowledge, skill, and understanding develop over time" (NGA & CCSSO, 2010, p. 4). LTs immediately reached a wider audience and became of interest to teachers and administrators.

At that time, a call emerged to "translate the available LTs into usable tools for teachers" (Daro, Mosher, & Corcoran, 2011, p. 57). This call implied that trajectories were perhaps not ready for immediate use in classrooms. As professional development (PD) designers, we were intrigued by the word "translate" and what it implied about connecting research and practice. We were interested in the "translation" process and how teachers would come to learn about and use LTs in their classrooms. We asked ourselves how LTs could be shared with teachers, which led to the development of the *Learning Trajectory Based Instruction* (LTBI) project.

Considerations about how to share LTs with teachers in ways that go beyond importing research into practice shaped much of our group's activities. We questioned not only how research on LTs can improve practice, but also how practice that uses LTs can improve research. We were interested in the opportunities LTs offered to connect research and practice, and like Silver and Lunsford (2017) suggested, we considered that this connection can be conceptualized not only as moving or applying ideas from research to practice, but also as a bidirectional exchange of ideas between these two communities.

From the very beginning of the LTBI project, we knew that the connection we established between research and practice had to be bidirectional. It is well known that the work of teachers cannot be reduced to the technical implementation of ideas created outside classroom contexts (Schön, 1983). There is also widespread recognition that direct implementation of ideas created outside the classroom is not an appropriate way to disseminate educational innovations (Elmore, 1996). Thus, PD plays a key role in connecting research and practice in ways that go beyond translation. As PD designers, we were aware of the importance of teachers' knowledge in any attempt to bring new ideas into classrooms. We were also aware of the impossibility of connecting research and practice without careful design that attends to teachers' contexts. Thus, the LTBI project was, from the beginning, a PD design project.

The work of the LTBI project was founded on intellectual curiosity about the processes of teacher learning. Researchers in the project were not developers of LTs, and our goal was to design PD on LTs that respected teachers' knowledge. The LTBI project took into account the questions we were asking regarding the connection between research on LTs and teaching that uses LTs. It was designed to generate knowledge about what teachers can learn in a carefully designed PD, as well as knowledge about researchers' learning when working with teachers in such settings. We were interested in how to build a two-way bridge between research on learning and classroom practice.

In this chapter, we discuss the conceptualization of the LTBI PD, the learning theories that guided the work, and the assumptions used in the project. We then describe the overall design of the LTBI PD across three iterations of the program and share a set of design principles. Next, we share how teachers learned to use LTs in professional conversations and incorporated LTs in their instructional practices. We also attend to the degree to which teachers' instructional practices were implemented equitably. Finally, we return to connecting research and practice and conclude with four claims regarding the design of PD on LTs.

DESIGNING PROFESSIONAL DEVELOPMENT
ON LEARNING TRAJECTORIES

Two important aspects of LTs encouraged the initial work of the LTBI project. First, the fact that LTs are recently developed, research-based knowledge about students was important. Designing PD around recently developed knowledge offers an interesting entry point for teachers and for the relation between designers and teachers; because the knowledge to be discussed in the PD is new and could not have been known before, the PD is not a "remediation" for lacking such knowledge. Rather, a teacher who comes to a PD about LTs is forward looking and interested in learning something that is at the frontier of research-based knowledge. This shift from one who lacks knowledge to one who actively seeks knowledge positions teachers as having agency when it comes to their learning. Second, LTs had a strong potential for becoming useful tools for teaching: they had a strong focus on students; were connected to standards, curriculum, and assessments; and explicitly acknowledged the important role of instruction. Thus, in the initial design of the LTBI project, we considered that LTs could be shared meaningfully in PD settings and had the potential to promote productive interactions among teachers and between researchers and teachers.

Designing PD around recently developed, research-based knowledge also has its issues. Conceptualizing how to bring new knowledge to learners is a design challenge because the knowledge is new and designers cannot build on prior teaching experiences with the topic. Further, trying to design PD around "new" knowledge, when the term "new" refers to knowledge from only one of the groups that is coming together in the PD, heightens the need to attend to issues of communication between the groups. For example, if LTs are tools developed by a different group with a different knowledge base and for a different purpose, what exactly should they mean for practice? The LTBI team was aware that "translating" LTs into usable tools for teachers required decontextualizing them from the settings in which they were created and re-contextualizing them in the settings in which they were to be used.

Learning Theories

Our thinking about the opportunities and challenges of designing PD for LTs was organized around two theories of learning: social constructivism and situated learning. These theories guided the initial assumptions used to create the professional learning tasks for the project. We briefly present these theoretical perspectives and then connect them to the LTBI design assumptions.

Social Constructivism. From a social constructivist perspective, learning is the active process of using one's prior knowledge and experiences to construct meaning of a new or problematic experience through social interactions (Cobb, 2007; Ernest, 1994). Knowledge is the constructed way an individual understands the world and thus cannot be directly transmitted. Because prior understandings and experiences are unique to the individual, they also cannot be reproduced. Where other forms of constructivist learning theories say little about the role of others in learning, from this perspective social interactions are central in promoting and supporting learning.

Considering teacher learning, social constructivism suggests that aspects of teachers' knowledge and practice come from resolving problems they encounter in their reality in classrooms and schools. Such knowledge is created in interaction with students as well as interaction with colleagues and administrators. To promote teacher learning in PD settings—a different reality—it is necessary to respect the knowledge from practice that teachers bring while creating experiences in which this knowledge does not adequately explain or address a new, perceived problem.

The LTBI PD was designed with the idea that experienced teachers have likely seen many of the strategies and levels of mathematical sophistication from the LTs surface in their own students' mathematical work. These teachers should recognize several aspects of the LTs, and their initial knowledge about these aspects needs to be respected. At the same time, LT researchers have ordered students' learning experiences in particular ways that attend to representing a mathematical goal over time, which may differ from teachers' organization of their knowledge. Therefore, the idea of organizing knowledge about students in a specific new way represents a challenge to existing teacher knowledge that needs to be addressed in the PD.

For the LTBI project, social constructivism offered a way to be respectful of teachers' knowledge while also thinking about what challenges would have to be resolved in the context of PD on LTs. We recognized that if LTs are tools that have meaning in teachers' practice, many teachers likely already know some aspects of these trajectories from their experiences with students. Therefore, our PD had to build from teachers' knowledge and help them reorganize it.

Situated Learning. From a situated learning perspective, learning is inherently social and a natural outcome of engaging in the social world (Lave & Wenger, 1991). It occurs in particular contexts as one participates in activities that are meaningful for a community. More specifically, learning is understood as changes in ways of participating in the community. Knowledge then, is valued participation in the community.

Considering teacher learning, situated learning suggests that aspects of teachers' knowledge and practice come from their participation in their school communities. It is in the school community that teachers are socialized into the profession and come to embrace norms about what it means to be a teacher. Schools shape the conversations teachers have about students and what is acceptable as ways to communicate about learners. Schools also shape teachers' expectations for student learning as well as expectations for teaching. Thus, when coming into a PD, teachers bring their ways of participating into the PD community. Situated learning also implies that the PD itself, particularly when it requires many hours over long periods of time, becomes a community with its own ways of participation, norms about being part of the group, and acceptable ways to communicate. Teachers participating in a PD community navigate between it and their school community to make sense of their learning.

With attention to communities, we designed the LTBI PD considering schools as the unit of change. To promote long-lasting changes in practices, it is important that what a teacher does inside the classroom aligns with the ways in which teachers participate in the larger school community. Thus, it is better when teachers are with their school peers in the PD, and there is overlap between the school and the PD communities. The LTBI PD was designed for participation of whole schools or teams from schools, promoting the development of a shared vision of mathematics instruction at the school level.

For the LTBI project, situated learning offered a way to design PD that respected teachers' contexts within their school communities. Because participation in this shared space shapes the identities of teachers and professional developers, all participants in the PD are learners who return to their communities with new knowledge and practices.

Design Assumptions

The initial ideas about working with LTs and the learning theories presented are the basis for several assumptions that guided the LTBI project. These assumptions have important implications for the design of the LTBI PD, and we summarize them before introducing the structure of the PD and the principles that guided its design.

Assumption 1. Teachers coming to PD on LTs are knowledge seekers and forward-looking; they have agency and make decisions about their own learning.

Assumption 2. Teachers' experiential knowledge about students' mathematical thinking has to be respected and challenged as they learn about LTs.

Assumption 3. Professional learning tasks to promote teacher learning of LTs are new tasks that require careful design thinking.

Assumption 4. LTs have to be contextualized in practice in the PD, and teachers' use of the LTs in practice needs to be supported.

Assumption 5. Teachers' participation in PD in school teams allows for stronger connections to the context in which teachers enact and can change practice.

Beyond these assumptions, the design of the LTBI PD also followed well-established recommendations from research on effective PD (e.g.,

Darling-Hammond, Wei, Andree, Richardson, & Orphanos, 2009; Garet, Porter, Desimone, Birman, & Yoon, 2001). This research has demonstrated that PD experiences that support teachers in expanding their knowledge of content and teaching lead to instructional improvements and increase student achievement share a number of characteristics. These experiences are intensive and ongoing, focus on teaching and learning specific academic content, involve collaboration with other teachers, engage teachers in active learning, and are connected to other school and district priorities and initiatives. It is also the case that PD needs to engage teachers in activities situated within the practice of teaching (Ball & Cohen 1999; Smith, 2001), that is, activities that use authentic artifacts from practice.

Design Structure

The LTBI project was a multiyear research and PD initiative funded by the National Science Foundation to investigate the ways teachers learn about mathematics LTs and how teachers use LTs in their teaching. The project also examined the ways teacher learning can inform the mathematics education research community about the usefulness of trajectories to teachers. To explore these questions, and to ensure the project created opportunities for researchers to learn from teachers, we developed and refined the LTBI PD program through three cycles of design, implementation, analysis, and revisions.

The first iteration of the program focused on the Equipartitioning LT (Confrey, Maloney, Nguyen, Mojica, & Myers, 2009) and was designed for K–5 teachers from one partner school. Twenty-four K–5 teachers from a diverse elementary school participated in the program. From that implementation, we revised the PD to include a more explicit focus on instruction, use LTs that related to a larger portion of the curriculum in any single K–5 grade, and more closely align with the Common Core State Standards. In the second iteration, the LTBI team partnered with a different elementary school in the same district, this time focusing on four LTs related to numbers and operations from Clements and Sarama (2009). Seven K–3 teachers participated in the project. For the third iteration, we worked with a different school district, again focusing on the numbers and operations LTs. We learned from the prior iteration that these LTs were more closely aligned to early grades, so we moved to a team-based model for K–3 teachers. Forty teachers from four elementary schools participated.

Although the number and distributions of hours varied slightly across the three implementations of the PD to accommodate local school and teachers' needs, the overall structure of the program remained the same. The LTBI PD was a 55-hour, yearlong program that began with a 30-hour summer institute, proceeded with 21 hours of after-school meetings organized as seven 3-hour meetings during the school year, and concluded with a half-day, 4-hour follow-up meeting the following summer.

Summer Institute. The summer institute focused on using LTs to examine and understand students' mathematical thinking and devoted a significant amount of time to the LT levels and vocabulary. The goal of frontloading the LTs was for teachers to become familiar with the terms and the ordering presented in the trajectories. Although the summer institute was quite intensive, teachers understood that the LTs would be revisited throughout the year to deepen teachers' connecting LTs to practice. In addition to the focus on LTs, the summer institute included attention to key instructional practices (Smith & Stein, 2011) as a way to elicit and respond to students' thinking. As teachers used LTs to analyze student work or watched video clips of instruction, frameworks to organize instructional practices around ideas from LTs were introduced (Sztajn, Confrey, Wilson, & Edgington, 2012).

Academic Year After-School Meetings. The after-school, 3-hour meetings (usually organized as three in the Fall and four in the Spring) revisited the LTs and focused on what was happening in teachers' classrooms as they began to use LTs in instruction. Although these meetings had a few previously designed tasks, their implementation was actually guided by an analysis of the prior sessions, teachers' questions, and events that emerged from practice. Teachers spent a significant amount of time discussing classroom tasks that cut across several levels of the LT to allow varied entry points, considering their students' thinking from a formative perspective, examining episodes and dilemmas from their own practices, and planning for subsequent instruction. These school-year meetings always concluded with a task for teachers to implement in their classrooms in preparation for the following meeting. These tasks were key for connecting the PD to practice. In the fall, the tasks focused on eliciting and interpreting evidence of their students' thinking using LTs, including conducting formative assessments of their students, engaging with students through clinical interviews, and selecting subsequent learning goals. As the school year progressed, tasks involved using the LTs to respond to students' thinking through selecting tasks, co-planning, and teaching lessons.

End of the Year Follow-Up. The final meeting occurred at the end of the year and included opportunities for reflection. This meeting was organized around classroom scenarios constructed from discussions that occurred during the year, and was designed to return to issues that emerged as important or represented a conflict. This final meeting was an opportunity to revisit and reconsider these issues from new perspectives and to begin to think about how to use LTs in instruction the following school year.

Design Principles

For each of the three main structural components of the PD, the LTBI team designed materials and professional learning tasks to use with the teachers (Assumption 3). We carefully considered how to engage teachers with the LTs, with one another, and with us as researchers. These efforts were guided by a set of design principles that built on our initial assumptions and were refined through the three iterations of the program. We present these principles and provide, for each, a brief rationale and an example of its use.

Principle 1: Representations of LTs

> Representations of LTs for PD purposes foreground students' mathematical behaviors visible during instruction; they offer multiple levels of specificity/granularity and connect closely related LTs.

Several representations of the LTs are needed for the purpose of PD. These representations differ in grain size and specificity, and they typically differ from representations created for research, assessment, or curriculum development. For PD, it is important to consider what makes sense to teachers, builds on their knowledge and experiences (Assumption 1), and is reasonable as a tool for practice when working with 20 or more students. In the classroom, it seems most useful to have representational tools that relate to what teachers can observe, are simple enough to allow for making sense of situations they encounter, and provide enough depth for subsequent reflection and planning activities.

Foregrounding students and their mathematical behaviors in these representations (Assumption 2) supports stronger connections to teachers' prior knowledge and helps to connect teachers' prior understandings to the new ideas introduced by the LTs. As teachers recognize their experiences in the LTs, they can further notice known mathematical behaviors from their classrooms. They can also begin to connect these previously known behaviors to new behaviors made explicit in the LTs to which, perhaps, they had not previously attended. A focus on students' mathematical behaviors also helps teachers transition between attending to the mathematical content of a lesson and thinking about how such content is transformed when students engage with it. This focus provides a structure for teachers to reorganize their existing knowledge in light of the new knowledge represented in the LTs, supporting the use of LTs in contexts where mathematical behaviors can be identified and named.

Whereas researchers may create one representation for an LT, it is often the case that one representation does not suffice to support the work of teaching. A representation that is simple enough to remember during the enactment of practice is perhaps too simple for the purpose of planning for next steps or analyzing student work; a representation that is useful for connecting across trajectories may not provide all the information needed to go in depth into the behaviors of one trajectory alone. Teachers use representations for distinct purposes, and they may need representations that highlight specific aspects of that slice of their work. For example, the focus on a single mathematical concept is helpful for assessment or unit development; when doing mathematics, however, students often use several related ideas and a representation of an LT for a single mathematical concept may not suffice for understanding students' thinking or leveraging this thinking to support further learning. In this context, a representation that shows several LTs across clusters of mathematical ideas and indicates how these ideas are connected is more helpful.

   A Representation of LTs in LTBI. In the LTBI PD, we created, shared, and revised several representations of LTs as tools for practice, including a representation called the LT Profile Table (Edgington, Sztajn, Wilson, Myers, & Webb, 2015). In our first iteration of the PD, we found that when students solved problems, they rarely used one mathematical concept at a time but used several mathematical ideas from different domains. Teachers, therefore, needed to simultaneously build from various trajectories and needed not only to understand one LT, but often needed to understand the connections across LTs. In subsequent iterations, we developed and refined the LT Profile Table to represent how several of Clements's and Sarama's (2009) LTs for early number and operations related to one another (Figure 2.1). Each column of the table corresponds to one trajectory. Each row of the table represents one learner profile, which describes the mathematical thinking of a hypothetical child for each of the trajectories. The cells of the table contain one or more levels of the LT associated with a profile. The cells are also labeled with a conceptual marker that describes and names a significant milestone for the behaviors in the cell.

   The introduction of the conceptual markers to the LTs serves two purposes. First, the markers promote visible behaviors indicative of an LT that we believe many teachers can recognize. Second, markers provide a means for "chunking" the LT. These chunks preserve the specific levels of the trajectory that are useful for understanding one student's thinking, while providing a way to consider more than one student's thinking. The learner profiles focus on students and provide a way of relating student thinking across LTs. As a whole, the LT Profile Table was designed for teachers to build the core ideas of the LTs from their existing understandings in the context of teaching and for multiple instructional purposes.

Principle 2: Professional Learning Tasks for Learning LTs

   Professional learning tasks for learning about LTs focus on students' mathematical thinking first, embed opportunities for discussing mathematics content, and utilize artifacts from practice. These tasks purposefully

sequence a set of activities that elicit, organize, extend, and apply teachers'
understandings of LTs.

The design of professional learning tasks sequences is a key component of PD
on LTs. Beyond designing representations of the LTs, professional developers
also attend to the organization of teachers' experiences around these representations and other artifacts. These experiences focus on specific aspects of the
LTs and are purposefully sequenced to achieve the goals of the PD. Regarding
elementary grades teachers, Philipp, Thanheiser, and Clement (2002) noted
that tasks with a focus on students provide an entry point for their learning
about students' mathematical thinking and mathematics content. These authors suggest that this focus connects more directly with elementary grades
teachers' knowledge and to how they approach their work. Thus, tasks to
support elementary grades teachers learning about LTs were designed to focus
on students first (Assumption 2).

   This entry point does not preclude opportunities for teachers to also
engage with mathematics content. It is not uncommon for PD projects to
first engage teachers with the mathematics of the tasks they are to use with
students and then connect this mathematics to students. Design Principle 2
reverses that order: It suggests engaging early grades teachers with students
and their mathematical work first and then using this context to bring forth
important mathematical ideas. Professional learning tasks, therefore, expand
teachers' pedagogical content knowledge and embed opportunities to challenge teachers' subject matter knowledge. These opportunities come from
finding the spaces in which students' mathematics bring forth important
mathematical ideas that challenge teachers' own knowledge (Wilson, Sztajn,
Edgington, & Confrey, 2014).

   Another key point for the design of professional learning tasks that promote teacher learning of LTs is to embed teachers' experiences in the practice
of teaching through the use of artifacts from practice (Assumption 4). Ball
and Cohen (1999) suggested that centralizing artifacts of practice grounds
professional discussions in students' mathematical thinking and creates opportunities for teachers to make new meanings for their professional work
that are closely connected to their practice. Further, Smith (2001) noted that
PD grounded in artifacts of practice can leverage and problematize teachers'
pedagogical content knowledge and their conceptions of students as mathematics learners. Thus, in PD on LTs, it is important for task sequences to
include connections to practice through artifacts such as video clips of instruction, sample student work, or assessment results. These connections
provide the context in which new ideas are introduced and experiences are
discussed and considered in practice.

   Attention to the sequence of the activities that compose a professional learning task is also a key design feature that follows from the project's

	Quantity/Place Value	Count	Add/Subtract	Compare/Order
	Perceptual Subtizing	**Cardinality**	**Use Small Collections**	**Matching Comparer**
Perceptual Child	• Maker of small collection • Perceptual subtizer to 4 then 5	• Reciter (10) • Corresponder) • Counter Small Number • Counter to 10 • Producer to 5	• Small number • Find result (add to, put together/take apart with direct modeling, counting all; take away using subjects)	• First-second ordinal counter • Nonverbal comparer similar and dissimilar items • Matching comparer • Counting comparer same size
	Conceptual Subtizing and Composing to 10	**Flexible Number Sequence**	**Direct Modeling**	**Counting Comparer**
Counting and Modeling Child	• Conceptual subtizer to 5 then 10 • Composer 4, 5, 7 then 10 (knows number combinations, doubles to 10)	• Counter and producer to 10+ • Counter backward from 10 • Counter from N (N+1, N-1) • Skip counter by 10s to 100 • Counter to 100 • Skip counter (counts by fives and twos with understanding) • Counter of imagined items (counts mental images of objects)	• Making it N (adds on to make another number) • Find change (find missing addend using objects) • Add to—count all • Take from—count all • Match—count rest	• Mental number line to 5 • Counting comparer to 5 • Ordinal counter • Spatial estimator • Counting comparer to 10

Source: Edgington et al., 2015

perspectives on learning. The sequence begins with an activity that elicits teachers' existing knowledge about students' mathematical thinking to challenge and create a need for new ideas from the LTs. Next, the sequence includes an activity where teachers discuss their ideas about students' thinking with the goal of teachers promoting and supporting one another's learning as they relate and organize their understandings. To extend teachers' knowledge, a third activity introduces LT levels as knowledge from the research community to provide structure and offer new ideas for teachers' discussions. The sequence ends with an activity in which teachers use their new knowledge of LTs in a practice-based experience.

A Professional Learning Task for Learning LTs in LTBI. For the LTBI summer institute, we designed several professional learning tasks to introduce specific levels of a trajectory. These tasks begin with teachers sharing their knowledge about a specific student's mathematical behavior, then teachers examine records of student thinking, and next their observations are formalized with the introduction of an LT level. The final activity in the sequence provides an opportunity for teachers to use the LT level to analyze written work or interviews with students, or to investigate their curricular materials.

For example, we introduced the initial levels of the Number and Operations LTs (Clements & Sarama, 2009) by posing the question, "What does it mean to count?" and viewing two short videos of clinical interviews of students counting sets of candies, with only one child demonstrating cardinality (Fosnot & Dolk, 2001). After teachers shared their observations and thoughts on what it means to count, we introduced a longer clinical interview of a student learning to count. To guide small groups' explorations of the interview, we posed the question, "Can this student count?" When sharing ideas from their discussions with the whole group, teachers noted ideas like one-to-one correspondence and rote counting. We then shared levels of the LT, providing vocabulary to label the ideas teachers identified and introduced other concepts from the levels, such as cardinality and subitizing. As a final activity in the sequence, we viewed the video again and asked teachers to use the (newly learned) vocabulary from the LT to describe what the student was doing.

Principle 3: Professional Learning Tasks for Learning to Use LTs

> Professional learning tasks for learning to use LTs in practice focus on supporting teachers in planning for, enacting, and reflecting on teaching using LTs. These tasks are purposefully sequenced to increase the number and complexity of the practices in which teachers engage over time while decreasing the support teachers receive.

It is important to consider how to support teachers as they begin to use the knowledge learned in the PD in their practice. Tasks that support teachers' use of the LT focus on key pedagogical practices that decompose teaching. They start with attention to a few practices, and over time the tasks include more practices and increase in complexity. For example, these tasks start with attention to how to elicit students' thinking, and later engage teachers in using LTs to plan instruction that takes such thinking into account (e.g., selecting learning goals and tasks, anticipating students' next answer). These tasks often involve teams of teachers working together in cycles of eliciting, planning, and implementing instruction around students' thinking.

This principle highlights the importance of supporting teachers in using LTs as a basis for instructional decisions. It includes the use of instructional practices that offer teachers opportunities to use LTs to elicit student thinking, such as selecting instructional tasks and posing questions while monitoring small-group explorations. Professional learning tasks that promote the use of LTs when enacting practices that require interpretations of students' thinking, such as examining students' written work, are also important, as well as tasks that ask teachers to organize instruction to advance student learning by leading mathematics discussions. These tasks are designed for teachers to find LTs useful in accomplishing their goals for teaching.

Similar to Principle 2, these professional learning tasks are intentionally ordered during the academic year to become more complex and include fewer supports. Regarding complexity, tasks first focus on practices where LTs are useful for eliciting and interpreting evidence of student thinking but do not demand an immediate response. As the PD program progresses, tasks expand to include practices that create opportunities for using student thinking to guide instruction. By the end of the academic year, tasks encompass a variety of instructional practices where LTs are used to organize instruction, respond to student thinking during teaching, and reflect on practice. Regarding support, these tasks start with strong scaffolds, such as providing teachers with tasks to try with one student, and over time encourage teachers to become more independent. For example, teachers may first implement a lesson that was collectively planned before being asked to plan and implement their own lesson.

This principle recognizes that instructional practices are important for the teaching community as teachers engage in cycles that begin with collaborative planning. In these tasks, teachers work together and use LTs to anticipate what their students know, how they will use that knowledge to engage with the task or lesson, and how they will elicit emerging ways of thinking from students. Teachers then collectively debrief what their students knew and how they engaged, reflect on their instructional decisions and ways they might have shaped student learning, and consider how the LTs helped them understand and build from student thinking. Through these cycles of professional learning tasks, LTs become meaningful in teachers' own contexts.

A Professional Learning Task for Learning to Use LTs in LTBI. In the LTBI PD, we designed and implemented a cycle of professional learning tasks for teachers to use the LTs in conjunction with key instructional practices. These tasks began with teachers working together to use the LTs to make sense of their students' mathematics (first one student and then many). Teachers were then asked to anticipate how students would engage with a particular mathematical task and to plan their instructional response. Between monthly meetings, teachers enacted their plan. At the next meeting, teachers reflected on what they had learned about students, their instruction, and the LTs. As the school year progressed, these classroom-based activities became more interactive and more contingent upon students. During the first after-school meeting for example, teachers anticipated how their students might respond to an assessment task. Later in the school year, teachers created a plan for and interviewed one student. By the end of the school year, teachers planned, taught, and reflected upon an original lesson they developed using the LTs.

Between the summer institute and the first meeting during the school year of the second iteration of the LTBI PD, teachers gave their students a diagnostic assessment for addition and subtraction. Before the meeting, we asked them to use the LTs to review their students' work and to select five students to complete a more detailed portrait of their mathematical understandings. At the meeting, teachers shared their students' work, the students they selected for the portraits, and how they used the LTs in the process. For the next meeting, we asked teachers to use the LTs to develop probing questions and then interview two students to better understand what the students knew about addition and subtraction. As the school year progressed, the tasks shifted from using LTs to elicit and interpret evidence of their students' thinking to planning and teaching lessons.

Principle 4: Working Across Grade Levels

> PD for LTs offers opportunities for teachers to consider student learning within and across grade levels.

A key consideration of our work is that schools are the main unit of change (Assumption 5), and as such, PD on LTs needs to consider work across grade levels to bring teachers from different grades into conversations about student thinking and how students' understanding of mathematics unfolds over time. This attention to several grade levels aligns with the mathematical scope of the LTs, which cuts across grade levels to examine how students develop their knowledge in large mathematical corridors. It is always the case that teachers, at any grade level, will deal with variation in student knowledge in their classrooms. This variation makes sense from the perspective of LTs but does not fit well with a grade-level structure that "assigns" mathematical ideas from the LT to different grade levels. Teachers who focus on student thinking are often considering mathematical ideas from several grade levels and working across grade levels can be beneficial. When teachers collectively examine student mathematical work across grade levels, they can learn to attend to the details of student thinking and develop an understanding of the relative sophistication of students' strategies, which is key for making sense of LTs.

Working across grade levels also promotes vertical alignment within schools. A long-term, shared vision for mathematics teaching and learning that guides the whole school community facilitates a way of participating that supports teachers and students in becoming a mathematical community. This grade-independent, common vision of mathematics teaching and learning promotes a coherent message about what it means to productively participate in mathematics lessons. Having teachers from across grade levels engage with student thinking together and consider learning as it develops over time supports a valuable alignment regarding mathematics teaching and learning at the school.

Both across and within grade-level discussions take place in small-group work during PD. Small-group work is key to giving all teachers opportunities to engage with tasks and discuss their ideas with colleagues. Small groups are the space in which most PD conversations occur and most teachers have opportunities to share their ideas and listen to the ideas of their colleagues. Thus, grouping teachers across and within grades purposefully is important for PD. For example, tasks using LTs to examine curricular materials or plan instruction provide opportunities for grade-level groups to explore variations in students' thinking in depth and share strategies for eliciting and building from this thinking. Tasks focusing on specific LT levels, on the other hand, encourage across-grade discussions about the evolution of a mathematical concept and how instruction at various grade levels or about specific parts of the LT supports student development.

Another way to promote and support work across grade levels is to engage teachers in examining tasks that offer multiple entry points for students. These tasks support instruction using LTs, and at the same time, examining such tasks also engages teachers from different grade levels who can use similar tasks. Having teachers from several grade levels consider similar tasks with multiple entry points promotes conversations about how different students can approach the task, creating an array of possible solutions that can be examined for their mathematical sophistication at varying levels in the trajectories. These tasks and the professional conversations they generate also support teachers in productively working with the existing variation in student thinking within their own classrooms.

Working Across Grade Levels in LTBI. In the LTBI summer institute, teachers worked in multiple grade-level groups on sequences of professional learning tasks focused on LT levels. This format allowed teachers from different grade levels to share their existing, and potentially different, understandings of students' mathematical thinking and focus on how that thinking matures over time through instruction. For example, the LTBI task sequence for the LT for Addition and Subtraction (Clements & Sarama, 2009) began by engaging groups of K–3 teachers in a discussion of different types of addition and subtraction problems and the strategies students use to solve them. For the next task in the sequence, the groups evaluated a set of instructional tasks to determine if they are useful in eliciting student thinking and anticipated how students at different grade levels would solve the problem. While presenting the LT for Addition and Subtraction to extend teachers' knowledge, groups viewed and discussed recordings of student interviews illustrating the different LT levels. For the final task, the groups used the LT to revisit their earlier anticipations. Across this sequence, teachers from different grade levels contributed to discussions about students typical of their grade level and learned from others how students once thought about addition and subtraction or how their instruction contributed to the growth of student understanding as a child moves through the elementary grades.

Principle 5: Setting Discursive Norms

> PD for LTs establishes discursive norms that use LTs to discuss students, student thinking, and teaching from a strengths-based perspective.

This principle highlights the important role of language as a tool for developing shared meanings when different communities come together. Introducing vocabulary for students' mathematical strategies and thinking in PD provides a means for teachers to identify, describe, and discuss students' mathematics (Goldsmith & Schifter, 1997). Providing specific terms for students' mathematics from research on LTs recognizes and validates what teachers often recognize as interesting aspects of students' mathematical activity and provides a way for researchers and teachers to share and generate new meanings. Most important, providing this shared vocabulary about students' mathematics creates a space in which teachers share their experiences and have new ways to talk about students and teaching.

The research and teaching communities have different discourses and distinct norms for discussing teaching and learning. The PD literature highlights the importance of establishing and maintaining clear norms to ensure that professional discussions of teaching, learning, and students are productive (Edgington et al., 2015; Van Zoest & Stockero, 2012). This discourse focuses on what students know and can do. Thus, discursive norms need to be clearly set, particularly at a time when deficit perspectives and the language of differentiated instruction (such as having "high," "medium," and "low" children) to express ideas about students learning have become normalized.

Setting Discursive Norms in LTBI. Considering the differences between communities and the importance of developing a shared discourse in bringing them together, we designed the LTBI PD to focus explicitly on developing a shared discourse guided by a set of norms for discussing students' mathematics (Edgington et al., 2015). During the first iteration, we successfully established and maintained ways to respectfully discuss teaching when viewing videos of classroom instruction. However, we found that when teachers viewed student work samples or recordings of interviews with students, many of the teachers did not use the LTs when discussing student thinking—in fact, many did not focus on students' thinking at all. In some cases, teachers commented on aspects of the task or the influence of the interviewer. In other cases, they used characteristics of the student to make claims about what the student knew or did not know. For the subsequent iterations, we developed a set of norms outlining how we hoped to discuss students' mathematics in the PD: describe what students can do; provide evidence for claims about what students do and do not know; develop hypotheses about the mathematical reasoning for the work students do; and recognize when statements are speculations or judgments. We introduced the norms during the first meeting and explained that LTs provide a way of understanding the mathematical thinking behind what students do, say, and understand.

TEACHERS LEARNING THE LTs IN THE PROFESSIONAL DEVELOPMENT

We now turn to our question concerning how teachers learn about LTs. Central to the LTBI PD design was an assumption that teacher learning occurs in, and is sustained by, professional communities. As we considered how teachers learned LTs in the LTBI PD, we were interested in understanding the ways teachers' participation in discussions about students' mathematical thinking changed as they learned about LTs. Through an examination of discussions from the first iteration of the LTBI PD, we found that learning about LTs led to changes in the ways teachers discussed students, but some of these changes were unexpected and troubling (Wilson, Sztajn, Edgington, Webb, & Myers, 2917). After revising the PD, we repeated our analysis and found that, by designing for additional aspects of the learning environment, teachers' learning about LTs led to more productive discussion about students as mathematics learners.

Discussions of Students' Mathematics in Iteration 1

From the beginning of the summer institute, a number of patterns in the ways teachers explained students' mathematical performance emerged in the LTBI community. These patterns often focused on who the student was (or was not) and what students could not do mathematically. These early discussions referred to students as being "low" or "high," or functioning "below," "at," or "above" grade level, and these descriptions were presented as accepted explanations for students' mathematical performance. We conjectured that learning about LTs would provide teachers with more productive ways of discussing students' thinking because they would gain new vocabulary to describe students' mathematics. Over time, it became clear that although teachers came to use LTs in their discussions, explanations that relied on student characteristics unrelated to mathematics persisted throughout the entire PD program.

At the conclusion of this iteration, our research team worked to understand how teachers' learning about LTs related to their uses of these explanations about students' mathematical performance by analyzing discussions from 21 professional learning tasks focusing on students' mathematics. We identified and defined four categories of explanations teachers gave for students' mathematical performance. One category explained a student's performance as being determined by his or her age or grade level. An example of this age/grade explanation is, "I would have expected that from the third grader." Another type of explanation used perceived ability, such as "high AIG [academically and intellectually gifted] students," "special ed [students]," "math whizzes," "my top kid," and "below level." Explanations also referred to amount of effort that a student had put forth and the degree to which a student was lucky in getting the correct answer.

Across the discussions from the 21 professional learning tasks, we identified and coded 322 instances where a teacher used one of these explanations when discussing students' mathematics. We also coded these instances to verify whether teachers used the LT vocabulary as a part of their explanation. Quantitative analyses showed that, as the PD progressed, teachers continued to use all four explanations in their conversations about students. However, teachers increased their use of LT vocabulary in conversations where age/grade or ability were used as explanations for students' mathematics. In other words, teachers continued to use age/grade and ability but used LT language in these explanations.

To better understand what these results meant, we looked across the 322 instances and identified 85 episodes in which teachers engaged in group discussions about age/grade or ability. For these episodes, we created qualitative summaries and then examined them across time. For discussions focused on age/grade, the increased use of the LT represented changes in the ways teachers' explanations positioned students as mathematics learners. As the PD progressed, explanations suggesting a student's performance was a product of her or his age or grade level changed, with teachers coming to use the LT to explain that a student's performance was less about maturity or grade level expectations and more about a student's prior experiences, both in and out of the classroom. In these discussions, teachers began to discuss how they could draw upon students' experiences as resources for their instruction—an idea highlighted in Principle 4. However, for explanations based on perceived student ability, the increased use of the LT did not result in changes to the meaning of the ability explanation. Teachers continued to discuss ability as an explanation for performance and integrated the new LT vocabulary in these discussions. Overall, learning about the LTs did not change or challenge teachers' uses of this particular explanation for students' mathematics.

At the end of the first iteration, we considered our findings mixed. On one hand, we learned that learning about LTs can provide more productive explanations for students' mathematics performance (age/grade). On the other hand, the results also provided an example of how learning about LTs and the use of LT vocabulary can reinforce the very explanation researchers had hoped to challenge (ability). Our team concluded that learning about LTs, without additional supports, was insufficient to challenge deeply rooted ideas about students' mathematical ability (Myers, Edgington, Wilson, & Sztajn, 2013). We then worked to revise the LTBI PD to include additional designs for two aspects of the learning environment. One, we modified the ways LTs were represented (Edgington, Wilson, Sztajn, & Webb, 2016). Two, we modified the discursive norms of the PD (Edgington et al., 2015). We conjectured the design of these two aspects would challenge and change ability explanations for students' mathematical performance by providing specific language to describe students' thinking together with specific ways to appropriately talk about students.

Discussions of Students' Mathematics in Iteration 2

In the second iteration, we introduced our norms for discussing students' mathematics and reminded teachers of these norms throughout the PD. We also used the LT Profile Table (see Figure 2.1) as one of the main representations of the LTs, providing more vocabulary to talk about students. At the conclusion of the second iteration, we repeated the analysis described for the first iteration to examine the degree to which the revised PD challenged and changed the explanation that a student's innate ability determines her or his mathematics performance.

As in our analysis of the first iteration, we examined teachers' explanations for students' mathematical performance, this time from 16 professional learning tasks. Using the same coding process, we identified 176 instances where a teacher used the age/grade or ability explanations. In addition, we coded teachers' uses of the profiles and markers of the LT Profile Table. We then used the same procedures from the previous quantitative analysis to determine if teachers' learning about the LTs changed the age/grade and ability explanations they offered for students' mathematical performance. Results showed that there was no change in the frequency of age/grade explanations, as in the first iteration. However, the frequency of ability explanations increased across the PD. For both sets, there was an increase in the use of the LT Profile Table over time. The results also suggested that teachers came to use the markers and learner profiles of the LT Profile Table when explaining students' mathematics performance. To understand how teachers' learning of the LTs led to these, we then looked across the 176 instances and identified 47 episodes in which teachers engaged in discussions related to age/grade or ability.

Findings for discussions that used age/grade explanations were similar to those from the first iteration. Teachers not only came to use the LTs in discussions of age or grade but, more important, the meaning of those discussions shifted from age/grade determining performance to one where a student's prior experiences explained her or his mathematical performance. For discussions with ability explanations, the increased use of the LT Profile Table coincided with changes in how teachers positioned students as learners. Unlike the first iteration, teachers' uses of the ability explanation shifted. Early in the summer institute, teachers' ability discussions focused on different "kinds" of students and suggested that mathematical performance was a byproduct of a student's ability. These conversations often included language where "smart" or "bright" students used correct and creative strategies when solving problems. After the first few days of the summer institute, teachers began to use the LTs to make sense of students' mathematical thinking. While these discussions continued to explain performance as a product of ability, teachers began using the profiles and markers in ways that suggested that students were sense makers of mathematics. In the discussions, teachers used the LTs to provide more descriptive explanations of students' mathematics. Halfway through the academic year, a different pattern in the ability discussions emerged and remained stable for the remainder of the PD. In these conversations, teachers used ability as a temporary descriptor to present students' current mathematical performance and used language from the LT to support these claims. As in the changes in explanations using age/grade, teachers discussed how students' prior experiences affected their mathematical performance, located students within the LTs, and used the LTs to discuss how they could respond instructionally.

These analyses of the second iteration showed that teachers' conversations focused on ability grew to view students' mathematical performance as temporary. With the addition of the vocabulary provided in the LT Profile Table and of explicit norms for discussing students' mathematics to the design of the PD, teachers were able to use the LTs to conjecture potential instructional decisions they could make to support student learning. Taking the two design modifications together, we suggest that when LTs are organized and represented in ways that centralize students as mathematics learners, and when mathematics PD designers explicitly attend to the ways in which norms are set for focusing and facilitating professional discussions on students' mathematical thinking, PD on LTs can offer productive ways for teachers to learn about LTs.

TEACHERS USING THE LTS IN THEIR PRACTICE

One of the overarching goals of the LTBI project was to understand the ways that LTs can be used to support instruction. We defined LTBI to be teaching that uses LTs to make instructional decisions and theoretically connected LTs to established frameworks for promoting classroom discourse within a student-centered learning environment (Sztajn et al., 2012). Thus, in each iteration of the LTBI PD, we sought to understand how teachers were actually using LTs as tools for teaching. Not only were we interested in the ways teachers used LTs in planning, instruction, and assessment, we were also interested in whether or not teachers used LTs to make more equitable instructional decisions.

In this section, we share findings related to teachers' classroom practice from the first iteration of the PD (Wilson, Sztajn, Edgington, & Myers, 2015), and results from a follow-up study with a subset of teachers from this iteration (Edgington, 2012). We then discuss changes we made to the subsequent iterations of the PD and highlight findings specific to issues of equity within teachers' uses of LTs in practice (Myers, 2014; Myers, Sztajn, Wilson, & Edgington, 2015).

LTs as Tools for Teaching in Iteration 1

To understand how teachers used LTs as tools for teaching, we analyzed teachers' enactments of instructional practices that were of focus in the PD. Along with the LT, we shared the student-centered instruction framework of *5 Practices for Orchestrating Productive Mathematics Discussions* (Smith & Stein, 2011). Our goal was to consider how teachers might bring together the two frameworks that we presented separately in the PD. In attending to these practices during the PD, we discussed the nature of open-ended tasks, anticipated students' approaches to tasks, and considered possible ways to organize whole-class discussions around students' mathematical thinking (Principle 3). Connections between the LT and the instructional practices were not explicit in the PD, and we communicated to teachers our goal of learning with them what student-centered instruction that uses LT might entail.

In the spring semester of the LTBI PD, teachers were asked to create and teach a lesson using their knowledge of the LT and their students. Teachers completed a pre-lesson questionnaire about their goals for the lesson and a detailed description of the task they were going to use. They also anticipated students' approaches and explained how they planned to organize their lesson. During Iteration 1, teachers' lessons were video recorded, and the teachers also participated in a post-lesson interview where they discussed the level of difficulty of the task, how they monitored their students' learning, and connections they wanted students to make. In both the prelesson questionnaire and the post-lesson interview, teachers were asked about the ideas from the LT they used in both planning and implementation of the lesson.

We analyzed these data qualitatively, and the results indicated that teachers integrated the LT and the student-centered instruction framework in a majority of the lessons. The LT supported teachers in specifying learning goals, selecting open tasks, and anticipating strategies and misconceptions their students might use. During instruction, the LT assisted teachers in focusing on strategies and students' thinking, not merely on whether or not students were "getting the right answer." Aspects of the LT allowed teachers to create opportunities for students to make connections across the various ways students were making sense of the task to advance the learning goals of the lesson. In all, the LT supported teachers in implementing student-centered instructional practices to teach higher-quality lessons. At the same time, the focus on the *5 Practices* provided space for teachers to make sense of the defining characteristics of the LT (Wilson et al., 2015). However, these lessons represented only a snapshot within these teachers' classrooms based on a purposefully designed professional learning task. To further examine teachers' practice, we followed up with a subset of these teachers to more closely look at how they used the LT in their planning, implementation, and assessment over time.

Follow-Up In the Classroom. Five 2nd-grade teachers who participated in the first iteration of the PD participated in a follow-up study to examine how they used the LT through three cycles of lesson planning, implementation, and assessment (Edgington, 2012). One researcher from the LTBI team worked with these teachers over the course of 3 months and, during that time, the 2nd-grade team collaboratively planned and individually implemented a set of lessons. Afterwards, teachers assessed their students' understanding, reflected on their lessons, and examined evidence of student learning to inform future instruction. Qualitative analyses showed that for these teachers, the LT offered insight into how to use student work to navigate student-centered instruction. First, the LT supported teachers in specifying learning goals and anticipating levels of sophistication among expected strategies. During instruction, the teachers used the LT to pay attention to the processes their students engaged in as they solved tasks. LTs also supported the recognition of important mathematical ideas that surfaced during instruction. However, the five teachers did not use the LT in the same ways or to the same degree. Figure 2.2 summarizes these variations in a framework that represents different uses of LTs for instructional planning, implementation, and assessment.

This framework highlights key issues to be considered when attending to the ways LTs are presented to teachers and lists ways to support teacher learning of LTs. *Emergent* uses of the LT are limited to the assessment of "what students know" as opposed to using LTs to design instruction that moves learning forward, taking students beyond where they are. *Initial* uses make connections between ideas highlighted in the LT and how students engage with open tasks and arrive at solutions to such tasks. Finally, *proficient* uses coordinate aspects of the LT with learning goals, expectations of how students engage with a task, and students' strategies and ideas that emerge during instruction to facilitate students' movement towards more sophisticated mathematical conceptions.

From the first iteration, we learned that the PD needed a more explicit focus on instructional practices throughout. We added scaffolds to our professional learning tasks, particularly those implemented during the academic year after-school meetings, when teachers could try ideas out in their classrooms and bring issues back for discussion in the subsequent meeting. These scaffolds can support teachers in moving from using LTs to focus on individual student assessment to thinking about whole-group instruction.

An important result of these two studies in iteration 1 is that not all "good" teaching practices are implemented in similar ways when teachers are using the LTs. While both studies provide "existence proofs" that LTs can inform many aspects of instruction in meaningful ways, not all models of instruction that emerged in our observations were to the benefit of all students. Therefore, we shifted our focus in the second iteration to question whether the uses of LTs in teaching supported each and every student, attending to equitable instruction.

LTs as Tools for Equitable Teaching in Iteration 2

In iteration 2, the LTBI team was interested in whether or not LTs provide teachers with agency to make equitable instructional decisions related to planning, grouping, and assessing students. To frame this focus, we followed Gutiérrez (2002) and defined equity as being unable to predict students' "mathematics achievement and participation" (p. 153) and their "ability to analyze, reason about, and especially critique knowledge and events in the world based solely upon characteristics such as race, class, ethnicity, gender, beliefs, and proficiency in the dominant language" (p. 158). This definition was useful to our study because, historically, equity in mathematics education has been reduced to studies about the achievement gap (Flores, 2007; Gutiérrez, 2008) or opportunity to learn (Elmore & Furhman, 1995). It allowed us to draw upon Gutiérrez's (2007) four dimensions of equity: access, achievement, identity, and power. Whereas the first two have been studied more often, equity in the classroom is more complex. Gutiérrez's dimensions

Figure 2.2. Teachers' Uses of LTs to Support Student-Centered Instruction (Edgington, 2012)

		Emergent Uses	Initial Uses	Proficient Uses
Planning	**Task and Learning Goals**	• Selects open-ended tasks • Tasks are used for assessment purposes only	• Selects open tasks • Chooses short-term goals in relation to long-term mathematical goals detailed in the LT	• Selects open tasks • Chooses short-term goals in relation to long-term mathematical goals detailed in the LT • Coordinates among proficiency levels in the LT to adjust tasks based on students' understanding
	Anticipating	• No anticipation in relation to the LT	• Anticipates likely strategies and misconceptions from the LT	• Anticipates likely strategies and misconceptions from the LT • Relates the anticipated strategies and misconceptions to learning goals detailed in the LT • Anticipates levels of sophistication among students' approaches as highlighted in the LT
Instruction	**Monitoring**	• Monitors for holistic descriptions of students' work as right or wrong	• Focuses on students' solution processes • Monitors for known strategies and misconceptions from the LT • Elicits evidence of student thinking by asking probing questions	• Focuses on students' solution process • Recognizes levels of sophistication among strategies from the LT • Helps students make connections to move towards the goals of the lesson • Asks probing questions to elicit evidence of knowledge • Recognizes important mathematical ideas from the LT beyond the goals of the lesson

Figure 2.2. Teachers' Uses of LTs to Support Student-Centered Instruction (Edgington, 2012)

		Emergent Uses	Initial Uses	Proficient Uses
Instruction	**Whole-group discussion**	• Focuses on student work as right or wrong • Ideas are often shared without consideration to underlying concepts	• Focuses on process related to known strategies and misconceptions • Inconsistently provides opportunities to make connections among approaches and important mathematical concepts	• Focuses on process in relation to known strategies and misconceptions from the LT, with levels of sophistication in mind • Provides explicit opportunities to make connections among approaches and important mathematical ideas from the LT
Assessment	**Evidence of student knowledge**	• Success of a task based on students' ability to complete the task	• Uses the process as evidence of knowledge • Uses language from the LT to describe students' mathematical work	• Uses the process as evidence of knowledge in relation to goals for the lesson • Uses the LT to consider a range of student knowledge present in a classroom
	Role of Instruction	• Views the LT for assessment purposes only	• Begins to notice key ideas from the LT as opportunities are provided for students to share their thinking	• Draws upon the LT to structure whole-class discussions to provide opportunities for students to consider more sophisticated conceptions • Uses the LT to inform specific questions geared to make students thinking visible and move student thinking forward

allowed for the examination of the more dominant views of equity together with a a critical perspective.

Given our assumptions, design principles, and prior work with teachers, we entered this phase of the study with a number of conjectures about the ways in which teachers could use LTs equitably. For example, we encourage teachers using LTBI to use tasks with multiple entry levels, thus allowing students with different mathematical understandings to engage with the task. Reflecting on this practice in light of the equity dimensions, we considered that this use of multiple entry points can provide access for students and may even affirm their identity. This process of reflection and examination of several practices led to the creation of a table of conjectures (Figure 2.3) across the four dimensions; these conjectures identified what equitable LTBI (E-LTBI) could look like in classrooms (Myers et al., 2015).

The E-LTBI framework served as an initial conjecture for an investigation with four K–2 teachers during the spring session of LTBI iteration 2. Prior to engaging in this study, the four teachers had already participated in 40 hours of the LTBI PD (30 hours in the summer and 10 during the fall semester). Although we did not explicitly define or discuss equity in the PD, we were challenging teachers to reframe their language about students during this iteration. For example, as previously mentioned, when teachers referred to students as "low" or "high" we referred them back to the LT to use language that focused on what a student produced mathematically as opposed to a "label" for a student. One member of the LTBI team observed these teachers (two kindergarten teachers and two 1st-grade teachers) for 4 months to fully understand how the teachers used LTs with each student (Myers, 2014). Teachers created mathematical portraits for each of their students and shared how they assessed individual students' development over time. They also participated in pre-observation conferences and post-observation meetings each time the researcher came to their classrooms.

This study provided critical information about the ways in which LTs can support equitable instruction. Each of the four dimensions was examined for uses in the classroom as well as for tensions it created. Most of the examples from the data aligned with the dominant perspective of equity, and there were data points across all eight indicators outlined in our initial table. These examples most often occurred as teachers planned for their instruction. Although some teachers were able to use LTs to select high-quality tasks, anticipate students' needs, and set individualized goals for students, other teachers' severe deficit orientations prevented this use (Myers, 2014). These teachers used LTs to talk about what students could not do as opposed to thinking about moving students forward. Most of the examples of the critical axis were found during individual work time and whole-class discussion. Of the 10 indicators in this dimension in the E-LTBI table, examples for only five were present in the observation of teachers' actual practices—leading to revisions of the E-LTBI framework. In practice, examples were observed in which LTs

Figure 2.3. E-LTBI Framework (Myers, 2014)

	Teachers use their knowledge of LTS and LTBI to:
Access	Design instruction and instructional tasks such that they are accessible for all students
	Identify and use up-to-date research-based materials and technology
	Be accessible to and attend to all students in the class
	Foster classroom discussions such that all students can participate and engage
	Provide all students with opportunities to engage in rigorous mathematics
Achievement	Set high, yet appropriate, academic standards for all students
	Unpack and build upon their students' prior mathematical knowledge and use it as a basis for understanding more meaningful and complex mathematics
	Select and use a variety of forms of assessment (e.g., formative, summative, projects, class discussions) to gauge student achievement
Identity	Support the achievement of a robust mathematical identity
	Listen to and consider students' out-of-school experiences and design instructional activities that incorporate elements from their homes and communities
	Validate the use of students' own algorithms and strategies to solve problems
	Assist students to build connections between the mathematics they learn and the broader world/society
	Encourage students to engage in mathematical tasks according to their preferences and participate in mathematical discourse in ways that are comfortable
Power	Ensure that students have a voice in the classroom
	Position students as experts in the classroom (this includes things they know in school and things they know outside of school)
	Allow students to solve problems that are relevant to them (these problems can exist inside or outside of school)
	Encourage all students to present, justify, and defend their mathematical ideas/arguments
	Help students to see themselves as sources of mathematical knowledge

supported some teachers in helping students build a strong mathematical identity, engage in mathematics in ways that were comfortable for them, and use their voices to steer classroom discussions. Other teachers did not believe all students had expertise or focused only on connecting mathematics to the out-of-school experiences of their "high" students.

The most important finding from this study is that, whereas LTBI can support equitable instruction, it does not guarantee it. LTBI alone is not enough to disrupt strong deficit orientations. Rather, LTs are a tool that each teacher used differently. For some teachers, LTBI can transform their practice, and reflecting on the E-LTBI table leads them to rethink their practices and beliefs about their students. However, teachers with strong deficit views can use LTs to reify their existing beliefs. In one case from the study, the LT was used to justify retaining a student in kindergarten. Therefore, we argue that a content-focused PD such as LTBI must occur simultaneously with PD focused on equity and challenging teachers' beliefs about students as learners. If we want teachers to use new knowledge of LTs in ways that benefit all students and provide focused support for historically marginalized students, focusing on content and pedagogy alone are insufficient: An explicit focus on equity is required.

LEARNING FROM PROFESSIONAL DEVELOPMENT DESIGN

In this chapter, we shared the design of the LTBI PD, including our assumptions and the principles we developed and refined over three implementations of the program. We discussed how teacher learning about LTs led to changes in their participation in the PD and described how teachers appropriated LTs in their teaching. We now focus on our learning as designers of the LTBI PD. In particular, we return to the discussion about connections between research and practice before proposing four claims that state our own learning as designers through this process. These claims are proposed as guidelines for future PD on LTs.

The importance of attending to and respecting teachers' knowledge, while also challenging it in light of new research findings, was at the core of the conceptualization and implementation of the LTBI project. From its inception, the project took the notion of "translating" LTs to teachers as too narrow and sought to understand (and establish) a bidirectional relation between research and practice. Border crossing was one of the ways Silver and Lunsford (2017) proposed to describe this type of connection between research and practice. They explained, "Border crossing draws our attention to the human actors and agents involved in the interplay between research and practice" (p. 38). Considering teachers and PD researchers/designers as "actors and agents" between research and practice, the work of the LTBI project engaged us in examining PD as border crossing. More specifically, in line with our situated learning theory, we came to conceptualize mathematics PD as a boundary encounter (Sztajn, Wilson, Edgington, Myers, & Partner Teachers, 2014). We claim that, from this perspective, PD around new research findings such as LTs can avoid a deficit view of teachers, and instead promote knowledge exchange between researchers and teachers.

As a boundary encounter, PD on LTs becomes "a premier space for researchers and teachers to exchange knowledge from their communities, impacting both researchers' and teachers' practices without reducing the importance of either" (Sztajn et al., 2014, p. 201). Because both researchers and teachers have valuable knowledge about students' mathematical thinking (as represented in the LTs and as stated in Assumption 2), PD on LTs is the space in which these different knowledge bases come together. Our situated perspective on learning suggests that knowledge is competence in the practices of a particular community (Wenger, 1998), and when researchers and teachers come together in PD settings, they bring with them their different knowledge about students—that is, different ways of engaging with students' mathematics. The PD allows for these two groups to cross the boundaries of their communities and create, together, what becomes a new, accepted way of performing. Developing a shared competent performance problematizes knowledge from both communities, and the new emerging knowledge can transform both research and practice. Participants in these boundary encounters take their renewed knowledge back to original communities, transforming those communities as well.

From a boundary encounter perspective, designers and participants in PD about LTs are boundary brokers who, together, create new boundary practices. They cut across communities, creating new ways to engage with those who do not necessarily share the same practices. These emerging boundary practices occur around boundary objects, which are representations of knowledge that can convey meaning across communities. In LTBI, artifacts depicting students' mathematics as well as representations created for the LTs (Principle 1) served as boundary objects, promoting interactions among researchers and practitioners. The design of tasks and participation structures to foster such interactions, however, cannot be understated (Principles 2–5). These tasks are created to bring forth and transform knowledge from teachers and researchers.

To conclude, we bring together our understanding of PD as boundary encounters with our attention to the purposeful design of experiences in this encounter to offer four final claims that represent our learning about PD on LTs.

Claim 1. Designs that foster teacher and researcher learning in boundary
    encounters around LTs take into account the contexts in which
    participants enact their practices and the existing discursive practices

about students' mathematics that participants bring into the encounter. These designs are intentional in the forms of participation they promote and purposeful in creating opportunities for LTs to support the transformation of any existing, deficit-based discursive practices about students' mathematics.

Claim 2. Designs that foster teacher and researcher learning in boundary encounters around LTs attend to both learning about LTs and learning about LTBI. Together with representations about student thinking used to discuss LTs, these designs also use representations of teaching and allow participants to experience the use of LTs in the context of LTBI. Learning about LTs and about LTBI cannot be separated and occur in tandem and purposefully in the PD.

Claim 3. Designs that foster teacher and researcher learning in boundary encounters around LTs promote sustained interactions among both communities through attention to teachers' practices at different points in time during the year. These designs build on teachers' schedules and curricula and may necessitate the learning of multiple LTs to remain relevant and connected to practice throughout the duration of the PD.

Claim 4. Designs that foster teacher and researcher learning in boundary encounters around LTs include equity as a central tenet. These designs examine different ways in which participants bring inequitable mathematics teaching practices or dispositions about students into the encounter and do not assume that LTs alone become a tool for equitable instruction. They intentionally and explicitly use the PD as a space to challenge inequitable practices and dispositions and promote students' access, achievement, identities, and power in mathematics learning.

NOTE

This chapter is based upon work supported by the National Science Foundation grant DRL-1008364. Any opinions, findings, and conclusions or recommendations expressed in this report are those of the authors and do not necessarily reflect the views of the foundation.

REFERENCES

Ball, D. L., & Cohen, D. K. (1999). Developing practice, developing practitioners: Toward a practice-based theory of professional education. In L. Darling-Hammond & G. Sykes (Eds.), *Teaching as the learning profession: Handbook of policy and practice* (pp. 3–32). San Francisco, CA: Jossey-Bass.

Battista, M. T. (2004). Applying cognition-based assessment to elementary school students' development of understanding of area and volume measurement. *Mathematical Thinking and Learning, 6*(2), 185–204.

Clements, D. H., & Sarama, J. (2009). *Learning and teaching early math: The learning trajectories approach.* New York, NY: Routledge.

Cobb, P. (2007). Putting philosophy to work. Coping with multiple theoretical perspectives. In F. K. Lester (Ed.), *Second handbook of research on mathematics teaching and learning* (pp. 3–38). Greenwich, CT: Information Age Publishing.

Confrey, J., & Maloney, A. P. (2012). Next-generation digital classroom assessment based on learning trajectories. In C. Dede, & J. Richards (Eds.), *Digital teaching platforms: Customizing classroom learning for each student* (pp. 134–152). New York, NY: Teachers College Press.

Confrey, J., Maloney, A. P., Nguyen, K., Mojica, G., & Myers, M. (2009). Equipartitioning/splitting as a foundation of rational number reasoning using learning trajectories. *Proceedings of the 33rd Conference of the International Group for the Psychology of Mathematics Education.* PME 33: Thessaloniki, Greece.

Darling-Hammond, L., Wei, R. C., Andree, A., Richardson, N., & Orphanos, S. (2009). *Professional learning in the learning profession: A status report on teacher development in the United States and abroad.* Washington, DC: National Staff Development Council.

Daro, P., Mosher, F. A., & Corcoran, T. (2011). *Learning trajectories in mathematics: A foundation for standards, curriculum, assessment, and instruction.* Retrieved from https://repository.upenn.edu/cpre_researchreports/53/

Edgington, C. (2012). *Teachers' uses of a learning trajectory to support attention to students' mathematical thinking* (Unpublished doctoral dissertation). North Carolina State University, Raleigh, NC.

Edgington, C., Sztajn, P., Wilson, P. H., Myers, M., & Webb, J. (2015). Norms for discussing students' mathematics in professional development. *Journal of Mathematics Education Leadership, 16*(1), 12–17.

Edgington, C., Wilson, P. H., Sztajn, P., & Webb, J. (2016). Translating learning trajectories into useable tools for teachers. *Mathematics Teacher Educator, 5*(1), 65–80.

Elmore, R. (1996). Getting to scale with good educational practice. *Harvard Educational Review, 66*(1), 1–27.

Elmore, R. F., & Furhman, S. H. (1995). Opportunity to learn standards and the state role in education. *Teachers College Record, 96*(3), 432–457.

Ernest, P. (1994). Social constructivism and the psychology of mathematics education, in P. Ernest (Ed.), *Constructing mathematics knowledge: Epistemology and mathematical education* (pp. 62–72). Bristol, PA: Falmer Press.

Flores, A. (2007). Examining disparities in mathematics education: Achievement gap or opportunity gap? *The High School Journal, 91*(1), 29–42.

Fosnot, C. T., & Dolk, M. (2001). *Young mathematicians at work.* Portsmouth, NH: Heinemann.

Garet, M. S., Porter, A. C., Desimone, L., Birman, B. F., & Yoon, K. S. (2001). What makes professional development effective? Results from a national sample of teachers. *American Educational Research Journal, 38*(4), 915–945.

Goldsmith, L., & Schifter, D. (1997). Understanding teachers in transition: Characteristics of a model for developing teachers. In E. Fennema, & B. S. Nelson (Eds.), *Mathematics teachers in transition* (pp. 19–54). Mahwah, NJ: Lawrence Erlbaum Associates.

Gutiérrez, R. (2002). Enabling the practice of mathematics teachers in context: Towards a new equity research agenda. *Mathematical Thinking and Learning, 4*(2&3), 145–187.

Gutiérrez, R. (2007). Context matters: Equity, success, and the future of mathematics education. *Proceedings of the 29th annual meeting of the North American Chapter of the International Group for the Psychology of Mathematics Education* (pp. 1–18). Lake Tahoe, NV.

Gutiérrez, R. (2008). A "gap-gazing" fetish in mathematics education? Problematizing research on the achievement gap. *Journal for Research in Mathematics Education, 39*(4), 357–364.

Lave, J., & Wenger, E. (1991). *Situated learning: Legitimate peripheral participation.* Cambridge, UK: Cambridge University Press.

Myers, M. (2014). *The use of learning trajectory based instruction in supporting equitable teaching practices in elementary classrooms: A multi-case study* (Unpublished doctoral dissertation). North Carolina State University, Raleigh, NC.

Myers, M., Edgington, C., Wilson, P. H., & Sztajn, P. (2013). Teachers' positioning of students in relation to ability/achievement in a professional development setting. In Martinez, M., & Castro Superfine, A. (Eds.), *Proceedings of the Thirty-fifth annual meeting of the North American Chapter of the International Group for the Psychology of Mathematics Education*, Chicago, IL.

Myers, M., Sztajn, P., Wilson, P. H., & Edgington, C. (2015). From implicit to explicit: Articulating equitable learning trajectories based instruction. *Journal of Urban Mathematics Education, 8*(2) 11–22.

National Governors Association Center for Best Practices & Council of Chief State School Officers. (2010). *Common Core State Standards for Mathematics.* Washington, DC: Authors.

Philipp, R. A., Thanheiser, E., & Clement, L. (2002). The role of a children's mathematical thinking experience in the preparation of prospective elementary school teachers. *International Journal of Educational Reform, 27*(2), 195–213.

Schön, D. A. (1983). *The reflective practitioner.* New York, NY: Basic Books.

Silver, E. A., & Lunsford, C. (2017). Linking research and practice in mathematics education: Perspectives and pathways. In J. Cai (Ed.), *Compendium for research in mathematics education* (pp. 28–47). Reston, VA: National Council of Teachers of Mathematics.

Smith, M. S. (2001). *Practice-based professional development for teachers of mathematics.* Reston, VA: National Council of Teachers of Mathematics.

Smith, M. S., & Stein, M. K. (2011). *5 practices for organizing productive mathematical discussions.* Reston, VA: National Council of Teachers of Mathematics.

Sztajn, P., Confrey, J., Wilson, P. H., & Edgington, C. (2012). Learning trajectory based instruction: Towards a theory of teaching. *Educational Researcher, 41*(5), 147–156.

Sztajn, P., Wilson, P. H., Edgington, C., Myers, M., & Partner Teachers. (2014). Mathematics professional development as design for boundary encounter. *ZDM Mathematics Education 46*, 201–212.

Van Zoest, L. R., & Stockero, S. L. (2012). Capitalizing on productive norms to support teacher learning. *Mathematics Teacher Educator, 1*(1), 41–52.

Wenger, E. (1998). *Communities of practice: Learning, meaning, and identity*. Cambridge, UK: Cambridge University Press.

Wilson, P. H., Sztajn, P., Edgington, C., & Confrey, J. (2014). Teachers' use of their mathematical knowledge for teaching in learning a mathematics learning trajectory. *Journal of Mathematics Teacher Education, 17*(2), 149–175.

Wilson, P. H., Sztajn, P., Edgington, C., & Myers, M. (2015). Teachers' uses of a learning trajectory in student-centered instructional practices. *Journal of Teacher Education, 66*, 227–244.

Wilson, P. H., Sztajn, P., Edgington, C., Webb, J., & Myers, M. (2017). Changes in teachers' discourse about students in a professional development on learning trajectories. *American Educational Research Journal, 54*(3), 568–604.

CHAPTER 3

The Children's Measurement Project

*Jeffrey E. Barrett, Megan H. Wickstrom, Jennifer M. Tobias,
Craig J. Cullen, Amanda L. Cullen, and Jae M. Baek*

We believe that researchers and practitioners should not operate in separate domains, but instead, "professional knowledge—comprising both scholarly knowledge and practice-based knowledge—must be *shared* within the community" (Silver & Lunsford, 2017, p. 42). For our research group, this commitment has translated into an ongoing dialogue with pre-service, practicing, and retired elementary teachers willing to implement, challenge, or refine learning trajectories (LTs) on length, area, and volume measurement. Indeed, our research group consists of a blend of researchers interested in children's measurement, children's thinking and learning of rational number, and the professional growth of teachers of elementary and middle school students. In this chapter, we describe our use of LTs as tools to coordinate practice and research in mathematics education. We begin by defining our use of the term learning trajectory, reviewing our goals for sharing these trajectories with teachers, surveying the historical grounding of our project, and describing our theoretical framework for design research in mathematics education.

DEFINING AND USING LEARNING TRAJECTORIES

A learning trajectory (LT) is, in general, an important tool for supporting student learning and for promoting good teaching. Our view of LTs aligns well with the first category of LTs as "cognitive levels" described by Lobato and Walters (2017) in their review of LT research completed since 2007. In this chapter, we use the following definition of an LT: a characterization of increasingly sophisticated levels of thinking, acting, and reasoning, directed specifically toward a substantially mathematical goal, with corresponding instructional sequences that provide a plausible gain in sophistication given any current level of thinking (cf. Clements & Sarama, 2004).

We have described specific LTs for length, area, and volume in detail elsewhere (e.g., Barrett, Clements, & Sarama, 2017). Here, we present a simplified portion of an LT on area measurement as an example, detailing the second level of an eight-level trajectory; this row explains "physical coverer and counter" reasoning and strategy (see Figure 3.1). Column one identifies actions a child may exhibit, the "LT level." The middle column describes our inferences about a child's thinking related to those actions. The right-most column describes misconceptions or partial conceptions evident at this level.

We envision LTs as useful guides for supporting and improving classroom teaching. This group of authors (based at Illinois State University) worked between 2007 and 2018 to develop and improve LTs as research accounts of children's thinking and strategies for geometric measurement. We have also encouraged teachers to use them as tools for formative instruction. In general, an LT serves as a tool to focus on a key idea, characterize increasingly integrated and sophisticated knowledge about the key idea, and integrate assessment items and instructional tasks to fit the key idea. The LT functions best when used as a formative assessment tool for clinical interviews with students (Ginsburg, 2009), both in research and for instructional conversations between teacher and student. It can facilitate a tutoring process with a group of students, or lesson preparation with an entire class; in each case, using the LT to isolate a level or two of thinking strategy helps a teacher (or researcher) pose questions that align closely with what the student has been doing or saying, prompting potential growth.

In the PD work reported in this chapter, our key idea was geometric measurement. Some of the researchers in our group were developers of LTs on geometric measurement, while others were focused on designing effective PD to bring research findings into the practical work of teaching. Our shared concern was to bring insights and tools derived from LTs to the forefront of our PD design. In this chapter, we share our conceptualization of the LTs as tools to benefit PD work. Next, we discuss our developing model for this PD project based in the implementation of the LTs. Then we identify our design principles and adaptive practices, emphasizing formative assessment as a central element to our PD. Finally, we discuss the productive tension between research-based accounts of student thinking on specific mathematical ideas, as LTs, and practice-grounded designs for PD centered on formative assessment.

History and Goals of Our Project

The LTs shared with teachers during the summer workshops discussed in this chapter were originally developed by Douglas Clements and Julie Sarama and later checked, revised, and extended by the Children's Measurement Project research team. The Children's Measurement Project was funded by the National Science Foundation in 2007, led by Jeff Barrett, Doug Clements, and

Figure 3.1. LT Excerpt Showing a Row from the LT Chart for Area Measure

Developmental Progression	Mental Actions on Objects	Anticipated Misconceptions or Partial Conceptions
Physical Cover and Counter (PCC) Attends to some aspects of the structure. *Tiling.* Completely covers a rectangular space with physical tiles. *Comparing.* Makes intuitive comparisons of two-dimensional regions with simple direct comparisons. *Places one sheet of paper over another piece of paper to select the sheet that covers more space.*	With perceptual support, can visualize that regions can cover other regions. With strong guidance from pre-structured materials, can direct the covering of that space and recognize that covering as complete. Can represent figural units as unanchored approximately rectangular shapes, aligning them (applied concept of collinearity), but often only intuitively and in one dimension (Mullet & Paques, 1991) or using height + width rules (Cuneo, 1980; Rulence-Paques & Mullet, 1998).	May not organize, coordinate, and structure two-dimensional space without perceptual support. *Quantifying.* When counting to a total, often relies on existing guides to direct counting but may count unsystematically in the interior. *Drawing.* When representing a rectangular tiling task, may initially draw approximate rectangular shapes, often leaving overlaps and gaps and often aligning only in one dimension. *Comparing.* May use superposition in addition to side-matching strategies when comparing two objects.

Source: Barrett, Clements, & Sarama (2017)

Julie Sarama. That group set out to characterize children's ways of thinking and understanding measurement in mathematics and science contexts. They also wanted to support instructional design in the curriculum and promote improvements in teacher knowledge of children's thinking for measurement in K–5 contexts. With this broad vision for research on student learning and

PD, we needed a comprehensive framework for the research that would cross the common boundary of research and practice. Thus, we engaged in longitudinal research with students, using LTs as a means to help teachers and researchers alike build comprehensive knowledge for teaching.

This research team expanded from 2007 through 2014 to include Craig Cullen, Jennifer Tobias, Jae M. Baek, Megan Wickstrom, and Amanda Cullen at the Illinois State University research site. This Illinois group addressed emerging challenges in conveying the findings from our research to classroom teachers. The detailed accounts and examples of LTs listed in published versions intended for researchers (e.g., Barrett et al., 2012) proved to be difficult for teachers to internalize and use in classroom settings. To clarify the ideas from the LTs, we began simplifying our accounts of students' mental models for thinking about measures, units, and spatial structuring. We also looked for ways to introduce the LTs to teachers without such detail, responding to the concerns expressed by teachers in summer and after-school meetings between 2007 and 2009.

Using a pattern developed by Clements and Sarama in their Building Blocks project (see Chapter 5 in this volume, especially the Building Blocks Learning Trajectory [BBLT] interactive website), we (the authors of this chapter) set out to convey the entire range of the LT research outcomes pertaining to grades K–5 to teachers near our campus. In their PD with teachers in the Building Blocks Project, Clements and Sarama provide an ordered collection of children's responses to tasks and ask teachers to establish rubrics for performance on the tasks. Later, teachers are given examples of children's responses with labels showing the LT level. They also provide examples of instructional interventions to prompt learning from each level to the next. Finally, teachers are asked to role-play various LT levels of strategy and thinking for other teachers to guess the portrayed LT level. These PD activities helped teachers learn the LT levels as categories to assess thinking and prompts for specific instructional moves. Following a similar approach, we used successive rounds of predicting and checking level claims between teacher participants and PD team members. We focused on brief video segments showing children at a variety of levels along any given trajectory, through task design exercises, and in discussion of sample instruction targeting specific levels of thinking.

Our group adopted a cyclical design process that is described in this chapter, over six rounds of professional development, spanning 8 years (2009–2017). Successive cycles produced less complex, more focused accounts of children's learning about measures of length, area, and volume and a model for lesson research focused on LT outcomes. As teachers participated in seminars, they were asked to contribute recommendations for simplifying the accounts of the LT levels, and over time, we selected and implemented their editorial suggestions. We balanced our attention to teacher's requests and our original goals.

We had three main goals for integrating LT research in practice. First, we wanted the LT to serve as a prompt for teachers to look much more carefully at students' thinking and reasoning about measurement topics. Next, we wanted the LT level accounts to serve as a guide to help teachers modify classroom tasks or develop new measurement tasks to fit their mathematical goals. Lastly, we wanted to establish support structures through lesson research (lesson study) to help teachers improve instruction on geometric measurement.

In 2009, a project team member conducted a case study of a 5th-grade teacher implementing the LTs through readings, mentoring, and a multitiered teaching experiment with two students (McCool, 2009). McCool adapted the four-part Cognitively Guided Instruction (CGI) rubric (Fennema, Carpenter, Franke, Levi, Jacobs, & Empson, 1996) to focus on topics in geometric measurement. This rubric consisted of an ordered list of behaviors useful to characterize varying levels of sophistication on number operations and counting, adapted to measuring length. She found that the teacher progressed from providing children limited opportunities to share and discuss their thinking about geometry to a level that also included responding to their thinking and encouraging them to collaborate and build up knowledge. She attributed the teacher's progression to the collaboration among researcher and teacher in the common pursuits of categorizing student thinking and designing appropriate tasks to support growth. These findings suggested principles for sharing the LTs with teachers in professional development.

Also in 2009, other team members (Barrett and C. Cullen) engaged teachers at a different school in a series of after-school meetings. The teachers and the research team members worked together sorting student work in relation to categories of sophistication (levels). They used written work samples the teachers had collected with brief written measurement tasks the researchers sketched out based on pertinent LT levels. The teachers agreed that they benefited from the opportunity to categorize student thinking and answers on written items using these tasks to elaborate on critical aspects of student thinking. It was important to those teachers that the LT levels helped them anticipate and interpret student thinking. It was informative for the research team members that these tasks served as linkages from the LT descriptions of student thinking to the instructional concerns of those teachers.

Both experiences shaped the design of the 2011 summer workshop for teachers. We learned that the teachers used the LTs as a way of anticipating a wider range of student thinking and to help them attend to students' strategies that were incomplete, yet relevant to their learning process. These teachers were attending to key mathematical ideas in students' incorrect work, something they said they rarely did. This helped them support students in completing/revising their strategies.

In the spring of 2011, we began a PD program with a cohort of 24 K–5 teachers. The program included 10 days of summer workshop, and 4 more days of lesson-study work in their classrooms during the academic year. A second cohort followed a year later. In 2016, we worked with a third cohort, focusing on the common conceptual aspects of the trajectories for length, area, and volume. In subsequent sections of this chapter, we narrate the processes we developed throughout this sequence of adapted programming for professional development.

Theoretical Foundation for Designing Professional Development

Fundamentally, we describe learning as an interaction between children's environmental setting, the activities they engage in through classroom instruction, and their own developmental patterns of reasoning and thinking, which we take to be innate, logical operations for making sense and developing language and thought. We posit that teachers gain sophistication in their practice through interaction with students, in coordination with their expectations about students' ways of learning based partly in the history of their own schooling, their interaction with peers in professional learning communities, and the foundational pre-professional instruction they experienced at the college level. Further, we believe teachers gain insight through practical opportunities to innovate and discuss difficulties they meet in practice.

Thus, we designed PD elements to support reflective attention to student thinking and afford teachers opportunities to experiment in their own classroom. We adapted tools and practices from CGI (Fennema et al., 1996) as well as from lesson study work (Fernandez, 2005), and selected guidelines and recommendations from the wider community of research focused on the use of student thinking to guide teacher development (Schifter, Bastable, & Russell, 2002; M. S. Smith & Stein, 2011). This commitment to learning by reflecting on student thinking requires opportunities to see what is possible through case studies showing real students in plausible learning and teaching situations. It also requires increasing the level of engagement with real students and classrooms, gradually helping teachers see implications of their instructional moves and decisions without all the ramifications of everyday responsibilities for teaching an entire classroom. In such a PD situation, there is still opportunity to make adjustments and corrections without an immediate consequence for a full class of students at once.

In keeping with experts on collaborative lesson research (Takahashi & McDougal, 2018), we argue that teachers need opportunities to engage with experimental instruction through study, planning, implementing, analyzing, and reporting on lesson outcomes and observational data. Thus, we designed PD that would support exploration of substantive tasks in classroom contexts. We assert that learning mathematics must center on the work of students meeting tasks—tasks that begin with contradiction, surprise, or argumentation—a real question for them (cf. Behr, Khoury, Harel, Post, & Lesh, 1997;

Weber & Lockwood, 2014). As we design PD, we think of LTs as tools to characterize and provide support for building an instructional approach to substantive mathematical ideas (e.g., measurement). LTs describe patterns students tend to exhibit as they interact with specific mathematical ideas. In the next section, we continue our discussion on PD design by discussing our overarching goals.

DESIGN OF PROFESSIONAL DEVELOPMENT

In designing PD, we envisioned the LT as a tool for formative assessment. Formative assessment refers to the idea that immediate classroom tasks and assessments can provide feedback and shape the instructional path for a particular student or an entire classroom on subsequent lessons (cf. Ginsburg, 2009). It not only illuminates what a student or class might be reasoning about mathematically but also provides information as to what instruction or task might come next and why. In conceptualizing formative assessment, Ramaprasad (1983) described three key instructional practices: establishing where the learners are in their learning, where they are going, and what needs to be done to get them there.

The Children's Measurement Project research team highlighted a parallel between formative assessments and LTs (Barrett, Clements, & Sarama, 2017) in that an LT can help teachers understand their students' thinking and respond appropriately. For example, let's consider a hypothetical 2nd-grade student, Henry. Henry's teacher has explicit learning goals for 2nd-grade students such as:

- Partition a rectangle into rows and columns of same-size squares and count to find the total number of them. (CCSS.Math. Content.2.G.A.2)
- Use addition to find the total number of objects arranged in rectangular arrays with up to 5 rows and up to 5 columns; write an equation to express the total as a sum of equal addends. (CCSS. Math.Content.2.OA.C.4)

His teacher must address standards related to area by helping students to see area in terms of same-size square units and using area as a tool to help them systematically count and attend to structure.

When asked to draw in area units to fill the space below, Henry made the following drawing (see Figure 3.2). He counted the squares by starting in the middle and spiraling out in an unsystematic fashion.

In considering Henry's actions, the teacher notices that he attends to some aspects of area such as covering the space with shapes. However, he has

Figure 3.2. Henry's Drawing When Asked to Draw in and Count the Area of the 4 x 6 Rectangle

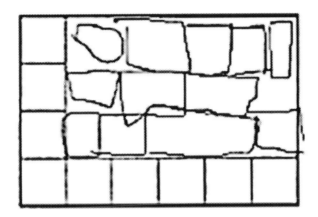

difficulty creating shapes that are similar in size, leaves gaps and overlaps, and does not know how to count the area in a systematic fashion.

In referencing the LT, Henry's teacher notices that much of Henry's reasoning could be captured within the Physical Coverer and Counter level in the trajectory (see left column, Figure 3.1), but she wants to assess how he compares and quantifies areas, as noted in the third column. She also notices that Henry may benefit from prestructured materials like physical tiles to help him understand area structure and counting strategies. We anticipated that the LT would help teachers like Henry's see what a student knows in relation to the learning goal and provide insight as to what tasks might promote growth.

The LT also provides rich tasks that support students across levels of reasoning in the same classroom. The teacher could provide a task, anticipate how students at varying levels of understanding would approach the task, and then connect students' responses. For example, two participant teachers used a task to measure the area of several gardens having the same perimeter, a task they had developed within our PD workshop. The teachers monitored their students and differentiated their support on this task to help students who held partial conceptions like leaving gaps or overlapping units (Wickstrom, Nelson, & Chumbley, 2015).

In planning our PD, we had evidence, from our own research and teaching experiences, that the LT held potential as a tool to assess and respond to the understanding of individual students (Barrett et al., 2012). We had also used the LTs to enact conceptually demanding, open-ended tasks. These elicited multiple student responses across several levels of reasoning (Barrett et al., 2011). Thus, we wanted to help teachers learn to use the LTs in these ways, and this guided our design of the PD.

Design Principles: The LT as a Tool for Teaching

Using an LT in instruction involves separate yet related tasks of teaching (i.e., developing tasks, identifying important aspects of students' work, interpreting students' understanding). We recognized that it might be overwhelming for teachers to address all these tasks simultaneously in PD. Instead, we offered multiple support structures to focus on these tasks both individually and collectively. Next, we describe the tasks of teaching using an LT from several perspectives and outline our plans for supporting teachers' use of the LT.

Prior research indicates that when teachers work with samples of student strategies to understand their mathematical reasoning, it can be transformative in their teaching practices (e.g., Clements, Sarama, Spitler, Lange, & Wolfe, 2011; Cobb et al., 1991; Schifter et al., 2002). Using videos of students working through tasks can act as starting points for teachers to wrestle with and understand students' thinking in a particular content domain. For example, the CGI project (Fennema et al., 1996) used videos of students working on number and operations problems as starting points in exploring students' thinking and possible instructional moves. Drawing from tasks in our research with students, we shared examples of student thinking and measurement tasks we used to emphasize important attributes of students' reasoning.

Our overarching goal of PD design was to help teachers use LT research as a tool to analyze and respond to students' thinking in productive ways. This goal aligned well with research on teacher noticing (Jacobs, Lamb, & Philipp, 2010). We adjusted our instruction during the PD to merge conceptual aspects of the teacher-noticing framework into our work. The three components of an LT (what students can do and say, what students are thinking, and instructional tasks appropriate to their thinking) align well with the three teacher-noticing components (attending to student strategies, interpreting student strategies, and deciding how to respond based on student understanding). We coordinated the components of LTs in our work with the teacher-noticing framework and derived four "tasks of teaching," similar to a framework by Smith and Stein (2011):

1. Designing tasks or modifying existing tasks to fit mathematical goals;
2. Identifying important features of students' work or actions related to a mathematical goal(s);
3. Interpreting students' understanding based on observing student products or exhibited strategies and their responses to tasks; and
4. Coordinating and categorizing student thinking to address different levels of strategies and reasoning in future instruction.

Although we used teacher noticing to help inform our PD design, we did not explicitly share our design decision to focus on noticing with participating teachers.

We used these four tasks for teaching to translate relevant research on students' thinking (the LTs) into classroom practices. First, we helped teachers develop resources and identify rich measurement tasks. Next, we asked teachers to identify features of students' work or actions in relation to our mathematical goal. Third, based on the tasks they provided and the goals they hoped to achieve, we asked teachers to pay attention to students' actions, such as how students used measuring tools, created and structured units, and quantified. In addition, we wanted teachers to study students' reasoning beyond level placement and wrestle with what the students' actions revealed about conceptual foundations of the measurement topics. Fourth and last, we wanted teachers to compare and connect students' reasoning with one another to find patterns of thinking and plan ways to prompt growth suited to each exhibited pattern.

In designing our PD content, we adjusted three dimensions of activity within the PD: (1) teacher role in classroom discussion, which we have called the four "tasks of teaching," (2) simulation of lessons versus actual lessons, and (3) varying numbers of students (i.e., individual, small group, or whole class). Here, we describe each dimension in turn, detailing the PD activities.

Teacher Role. When using an LT, a teacher takes on different roles. When choosing tasks and enacting curriculum, a teacher acts as task designer and evaluator (task of teaching number 1). After a task has been chosen, the teacher's role changes to observer as he or she attends to important attributes in students' strategies (task of teaching 2). After observing, the teacher's role changes to that of an interpreter as he or she works to make sense of what a student understands based on the student's actions (task of teaching 3). Finally, the cycle begins again and the teacher becomes a task designer as he or she decides where to go next, coordinating and relating student responses to form appropriate next interventions or tasks (task of teaching 4). We wanted teachers to have opportunities to practice these roles in a systematic way, integrating all four mindsets, but we also wanted them to engage each mindset independently.

Simulated Events. We wanted teachers to practice the tasks of teaching in simulated environments, prior to working with their actual students. Simulations are helpful in that they allow teachers to make conjectures about students' reasoning and pedagogical choices without consequence. We employed sample videos and written work where teachers were able to discuss what they observed, what they understood about students' thinking, and how they might respond pedagogically.

Number of Students. We wanted to reduce the complexity of formative assessment by working first with one student, then two, then a small group, and finally an entire class. Varying the number of students in this way allows teachers to move from noticing and responding to one particular student's understanding to noticing and describing multiple students' understanding within a small group before working with all the students in a classroom.

Professional Development Activities

When designing PD activities, we revisited the four tasks of teaching discussed in our section on design principles. In the sections that follow, we describe how we emphasized various aspects of teaching. We also describe several of the PD activities with specific examples (see Figure 3.3).

Pedagogical Supports. In considering tasks of teaching and perspectives on teaching and learning, we also found it was important to provide practical support to teachers. The LT provided information on students' thinking, but teachers needed structure in using this information to make pedagogical decisions such as designing lessons and tasks, facilitating discussions, or connecting student responses to categorize and assess thinking. We introduced the book *5 Practices for Orchestrating Productive Mathematics Discussion* (Smith & Stein, 2011) to help teachers improve classroom discussion. We included activities during our second round of PD summer workshops that focused directly on monitoring, anticipating, connecting, selecting, and sequencing students' thinking and responses. We also worked

Figure 3.3. Description of LT Tasks in Relation to Multiple Dimensions of Teaching

Setting	Simulation	Actual
Individual Student	Video analysis of individual case students solving tasks	Role-playing elementary student at particular level
		Interviewing students during summer PD at local summer activity center
Multiple Students	Round-robin video analysis of multiple case students solving the same task	Interviewing 3–4 students from teachers' classrooms
Whole Classroom	Observation of PD facilitators (researchers) teaching students at local summer activity center during summer PD	Teaching in own classroom
	Observation of other teachers during lesson study	

specifically to define and exemplify high-demand level tasks (Thanheiser et al., 2016). Lastly, we discussed ways of attending to variation in reasoning among students.

Individual Video Analysis to Highlight Partial Understanding. We used individual student video analysis each day in the summer workshops. It was a simulated activity focused on an individual student so teachers could consider one student's ideas deeply, as observers and interpreters. The purpose of this activity was for the teachers to become familiar with engaging measurement tasks, become attuned to subtleties in the ways students reason, and relate a student's reasoning to future instructional steps.

Individual Video Analysis Example. For this activity teachers were first given a task and asked:

> If you were to present this task to students in your classroom, what would be some strategies that you might expect to see? (Identify the grade level of your classroom and provide a thorough description of the strategies.)

Teachers were given 5–10 minutes to individually solve the task, brainstorm how students might solve it, and discuss their predictions with others. During this phase, we wanted teachers to practice seeing the content from their students' perspectives, anticipate students' responses, and infer students' thinking patterns. In the first few days of PD we had teachers primarily rely on their own experiences, so we encouraged them to explore the LT as a reference tool. For example, teachers were asked to consider how their students might compare the area of a 5 x 8 rectangle to that of a 9 x 4 rectangle. Many discussed counting squares, drawing in units, using the area formula for a rectangle, or mistakenly counting squares around the perimeter. For example, Angelica said,

> I think my students would count all the squares and then decide which one is bigger. Some might connect the lines and then count the squares. The more advanced kids would take the L x W to find the answer. My grade level is 4th grade. Some lower students might count the lines instead of the squares. Some kids might think it is perimeter and count the distance around the figure.

We asked teachers to sketch out a range of partial strategies, arguing that students often have some ideas and make partial progress that should be leveraged. Next, the teachers watched a video recording of one child solving the task and were asked to reflect on the following prompts, adapted from Jacobs et al. (2010).

- Please describe in detail what you think the child did or the strategy that he/she used in response to the task.
- Please describe what you learned about this child's understanding (what do you think the student is thinking and at what level of the LT would you place the student?)
- Pretend you are the classroom teacher of this student. What problem(s) or task(s) might you pose to the student next and why?

Again, teachers reflected individually on each of these prompts for 5–10 minutes and discussed their assessment of the student's strategy. During this phase, we wanted teachers to be able to share details they noticed, discuss student thinking in relation to the LT, and brainstorm alternate instructional pathways. We also chose examples that were complex; we wanted teachers to inquire about how a student's strategy might reveal his reasoning about geometric measures.

For example, we chose a video of a student who seemed unsure if he should count the corner squares of a 4 x 9 rectangle twice or once as he worked to find its area. The student began by counting the squares in the first column of the rectangle, one at a time, and reported finding a width of four squares (correctly). Next, he counted the squares in the bottom row, but he did not count the first or last square (the corners of the rectangle), reporting a length of 7 instead of 9 (incorrectly). The student paused without stating the area, perhaps wondering if he should multiply 4 x 9 or 4 x 7. Finally, he says it is 8 x 4, and says that is 36 units.

When asked to describe what the student did in the video, the teachers offered the following observations and claims about that student's thinking:

- He did not want to count the corner twice.
- He did not lay a tile down to count the corner.
- He multiplied 8 x 4 but his answer of 36, although it represented the area, did not match the multiplication fact.

At this point, the facilitators asked teachers to consider the LT in relation to the video to consider what the student understood and how to provide instructional support. For example, in this case, many of the teachers thought that perhaps the student had learned area as length times width (l x w) but did not know what it meant in terms of the tick marks appearing along the perimeter for both rectangles. When asked what they would do next as a classroom teacher, many of the teachers said they would give the student enough tiles to completely cover the two rectangles for counting or have him draw arrays of squares in patterns until he might discover the multiplication facts. Taken together, these responses from participating teachers correspond closely to descriptions of student thinking from the LT: Teachers noted that students have to understand structuring with individual units before they can build rows and columns, and finally they noted a multiplicative relationship should be connected to a figural array of squares.

We used individual video analysis to provide opportunity for teachers to discuss student thinking at a level of detail otherwise impractical during a school year, and we expected to invite their reflection. Many of the teachers began the PD saying that measurement tasks are simple to teach, expecting to fix students' struggles by replaying or restating proper procedures. However, seeing students' incomplete conceptions without knowing what happened next was confusing for the teachers; it prompted them to search for alternative interventions to support students. We realize teachers see many different measurement strategies within the classroom, so we wanted them to have adequate tools to identify partial strategies or obstacles as they occur. We also wanted to identify instructional practices appropriate for such partial strategies, or obstacles.

Round-Robin Video Analysis. The round-robin video analysis was an extension of the individual student video analysis. Teachers were asked to reflect on multiple students' reasoning and plan a lesson that would support learning for specific reasoning patterns. The teacher took on the role of observer, interpreter, and task designer. In the initial year of PD, teachers voiced that it was difficult imagining how they would coordinate instruction attending to multiple student strategies across the LT. In this activity, we simulated multiple students to give teachers time to envision ways of addressing different types of reasoning. Teachers were first told to solve a task and then predict how students might solve the task using the LT as a guide. Next, teachers rotated through five stations to engage with four other students, each exhibiting slightly different strategies. Teachers were asked to describe each student's thinking.

After visiting each station and taking time to write and reflect, the teachers worked in small groups to determine: (1) how the students' reasoning compared with other students' and (2) what task or problem they might post that would work for all the students across videos. Comparing multiple students' approaches to a single task often illuminated subtleties in the LT and helped teachers notice differences in the ways students could reason about the same task.

Student Interviews in Real Time. Next, teachers prepared and conducted student interviews with visiting children from a nearby summer activity center. The purpose of the student interviews was to help teachers transition toward work with students in an entire classroom during the upcoming academic year. The teachers were required to take on the roles of observer and interpreter while interacting with the students. It was important to have the teachers work one-on-one with students so they could practice asking questions and get a deeper sense of what each student understood.

In grade-level groups, the teachers selected or designed tasks and related each task to a level of the LT. Teachers often chose tasks we had modeled already, adjusting the tasks in minor ways. For example, we interviewed Mrs. Goldin and here report her description and purpose of tasks she included in her plans for interviewing students as preparation for the whole-class lesson.

> *Interviewer:* What are tasks that might inform the lesson and how will they inform the lesson?
>
> *Goldin:* I will use tasks allowing students to explore area using standard and non-standard units of measurement, along with the results of math screeners that will help guide the teacher in the development of future lessons on area.
>
> *Interviewer:* Please describe each task in detail.
>
> *Goldin:* First I will use a Conversion Measurement Task. Students are given a piece of paper, a one-inch square tile, and a pencil. Ask the student to draw a rectangle that is four times as big as the square. This task will help to reveal the student's conceptions about comparing area. Next, I will use a Partial Area Task: Given a rectangle that is partially covered by five squares along the diagonal, students need to determine how many squares total would be needed to completely cover the rectangle. That task will help show how students cover space and structure area. Lastly, I will use a Fixed Area–Missing Perimeter Task: Ask the student to draw one square unit. Once she has done this, have the student draw a rectangle with an area of 12 square units. The student should label the area and perimeter of her rectangle. If the student is successful, have the student draw two more rectangles with an area of 12 square units. Have the student label the area and perimeter of each.

After choosing tasks, the teachers first rehearsed an interview situation in which one teacher posed tasks and a partner pretended they were at a certain level of reasoning within the LT, using a strategy exhibiting that particular type of reasoning as if she were a student. In response, the interviewing teacher would try to categorize the LT level exhibited by the role-playing teacher and give a rationale for the level she identified. After a day of role-playing, teachers worked with small groups of students from the summer activity center to further pilot and refine their tasks. Finally, teachers were asked to describe the students' actions, thinking in terms of the LT, and possible instructional moves forward. The purpose of the reflection questions across PD activities was to encourage teachers to attend to details and use evidence when describing students' thinking and reasoning in relation to the LT.

Lesson Observation in Classrooms. Following interviews with individual students, and then pairs of students, teachers worked together to design two lessons that PD leaders would teach to a group of 15–20 students. The purpose of this activity was to give teachers time to take on the role of task designer but also give them the opportunity to observe and interpret students' thinking without having to teach in real time. In large teams, the teachers planned in groups, attending to the following questions (M. S. Smith & Stein, 2011):

- What are the goals of the lesson?
- What do you want students to know and why?
- Describe the measurement task.
- Based on your interviews, what level(s) of the LT should inform your lesson?
- Anticipation: Using the LT, how do you think the students you interviewed will respond to your lesson?
- Monitoring: How will you keep track of what students are doing and what they understand?
- Selection and Sequencing: How will you structure the lesson to address students' needs?
- Connections: How will you challenge students at multiple levels in your lesson and connect students' responses?

After addressing these questions, the teachers presented their tasks and ideas about the lesson to the PD facilitators, and two of the facilitators taught sample lessons using those tasks and ideas. While the PD facilitator taught the students, the participating teachers observed in the style of lesson study: Each teacher predicted, using the LT as a guide, how students would respond during the lesson, and then observed to check. Teachers were encouraged to focus on one or two students during the lesson, providing evidence of how the student(s) reasoned about the task. Following the lesson, teachers participated in a debriefing where they discussed the following questions:

- Was the task appropriate for your classroom? Why or why not?
- What did you see the students in your classroom doing?
- What do you think this means about their understanding? (If possible, what level of the LT categorizes their thinking and why?)
- What knowledge do you think that the student gained from the lesson?
- What might you do next and why?

The purpose of the debriefing was to provide support for teachers as they reasoned about students' thinking and instructional practices in relation to the LT. We had teachers work together to develop shared responsibility and to practice evaluating the thinking of students rather than the teacher's actions.

All of the tasks mentioned were in preparation for the tasks of teaching we expected teachers to enact during the school year. We wanted teachers to leave the PD with experience designing or modifying appropriate measurement tasks, identifying important attributes of students' work, interpreting students' thinking in terms of the LT, and coordinating and categorizing students' thinking during instruction. In the final days of PD, the teachers worked in smaller grade-level groups to develop interview tasks for their students and prepare a measurement lesson as task designers.

During the school year, teachers conducted individual interviews with 3–4 students from their own classrooms to inform their proposed lesson. Following interviews, the teachers met in grade-level groups to discuss how students' responses and understanding would inform instruction. Lastly, all the teachers taught the lesson in their own classrooms, but only a few teachers were asked to teach for the public lesson-study events. During the public lesson, the teachers and several PD facilitators observed and discussed the ways students learned from the designed lesson.

REFLECTIONS ON DESIGN DECISIONS

Earlier in the chapter, we discussed four distinct, yet interrelated, *tasks of teaching* we envisioned teachers enacting as they incorporated LT research into practice (designing tasks, identifying features of student work, interpreting students' understanding, and coordinating and characterizing student thinking). In this section, we review ways of using the LTs as guides to develop activities, looking through the lens of our own experiences and data. We begin by discussing content and task design. Then we discuss using the LT in relation to identifying, understanding, and responding to students' thinking.

Task Design: Emphasizing Concepts

Across all of our professional development sessions, we have noticed it is challenging for teachers to find rich measurement tasks from their curriculum or to develop these tasks that move students from simple counting processes into conceptual activities. In reviewing elementary mathematics textbooks, Smith, Males, and Gonulates (2016) found an inadequate percentage of tasks that foster a deep, conceptual understanding of measurement in the textbooks. In their review of three common U.S. elementary math textbook series, they found a dominant focus on procedures for geometric measurement in contrast to conceptual work. For the most part, we found that teachers in our project were working with tasks and curricula that highlight measurement as a step-by-step procedure to be followed rather than tasks that promote critical thinking about measurement topics. With this in mind, we challenged teachers to modify the tasks in their textbooks, which is a potentially uncomfortable and difficult position for teachers.

In our 2011 summer workshop with teachers, we first encountered challenges with existing curricula. When we were observing a 1st-grade teacher, she showed us a task in which students were asked to find the length of a flexible curved object, like a ribbon or a worm in its contracted position, set next to a ruler. A student would merely need to read off the number on the ruler near the end of the curved object without attending to the problem that the curved object would reach further along the ruler if it were straightened out. The teacher asked if the task should be modified. We asked her to reword it so the student would need to estimate the true length, imagining that the object had been straightened out.

In subsequent years, we provided teachers a wider collection of conceptually focused tasks. The teachers often accepted our tasks but seemed concerned that their students would struggle and offer partial solutions, as they had seen students do in the video segments we presented. Wickstrom (2014) documented the tendency for teachers to believe students understood measurement concepts because they knew and could enact a particular measurement formula. Many of the teachers were surprised when their perception of students' understanding did not match how students performed on the conceptual tasks. After participating in our PD, teachers were much more willing to employ longer, more conceptual measurement tasks, noting that their students lacked such a foundation.

For example, Wickstrom (2014) worked with Mrs. Effington, a 5th-grade teacher. Effington asked students to create several different rectangles with a fixed area of 24 units and to also make observations about perimeter. Mrs. Effington predicted the students would easily refer to multiplication facts to generate multiple rectangles, all with an area of 24 units. During the interviews, students did not rely on multiplication facts: They drew rectangles experimentally and rarely found shapes with an area of 24 units.

When met with discrepancy between what she thought her students knew and their performance on the task, Mrs. Effington worked extensively on a conceptually based instructional unit on volume measurement using tasks from our PD seminar (2012) with tasks she developed herself. In describing past instructional practices in teaching volume measurement, she reported that she provided students with drawings of rectangular prisms and emphasized multiplying the length, width, and height to find volume. Volume measurement was usually taught within 2 days with a focus on computation.

Later, Mrs. Effington decided she should not give her students the formula but give them physical models and allow them to generate ideas about how to calculate volume on their own. In response to what she learned, she created her own tasks in which students were given physical boxes, rectangular prisms, and asked to describe how they would find the volume. For example, her class was given a 2 x 4 x 7 prism and asked to describe how they saw and calculated the volume. She encouraged them to share strategies.

For example, one student described that she saw it like an elevator and saw 7 floors each containing 8 units (correctly). Another student said that he saw it like a waterfall and saw 4 slices of 14 (also correctly). Mrs. Effington questioned them on how both could represent the volume of the rectangular prism in different ways, yet correctly.

As she reflected on the unit, Mrs. Effington discussed the importance of letting students play with physical cubes to build prisms and understand structure. She noted that shifting her focus to the unit allowed her to see why kids needed to play around with the idea to understand it. Like Mrs. Effington, teachers in our project typically discussed a shift in their understanding of measurement content, either toward units as conceptual objects, or toward the repetition and grouping of measurement units (for length, area, or volume). Learning that there was more to understanding measurement and developing tasks than memorizing a formula took extensive opportunities to see students with partial knowledge playing out in ways that motivated the teachers to think about more engaging tasks, more conceptual interventions to support growth.

Teachers need resources to help them envision rich measurement tasks open to varied ways of reasoning. We have worked to address this need by working with classroom teachers to design a book of sample tasks related to levels of the LT (Barrett, Cullen, Behnke, & Klanderman, 2017). More resources are needed that address the complex interaction of progressive concepts on a continuum of measurement topics with appropriate task sequences to support students along that continuum.

Using Students' Mathematical Thinking

In Wickstrom, Baek, Barrett, Tobias, and Cullen (2012), we reported one case study with a 1st-grade teacher, as she participated in interviews with students, classroom instruction, and classroom observations. Through the lens of teacher noticing (Jacobs, Lamb, & Philipp, 2010), we found that the LT helped that teacher describe her students' thinking and notice conceptual aspects of measurement. When the teacher worked one-on-one with students or observed another teacher's classroom, she was better able to attend to students' strategies and provide interpretation of their thinking and reasoning than when she reflected on her own classroom lessons. This initial case challenged us to consider the tools and supports teachers would need to effectively integrate knowledge of LTs into practice and the teacher's role in using an LT.

Wickstrom (2014) documented the process of supporting changes in practice through the implementation of LT research in classroom instruction with three teachers across a school year. The teachers used the LTs to design or modify instruction for their classroom as a rubric for formative assessment, or sometimes as a source of increasingly sophisticated sets of tasks. These teachers used the LT to help filter their observations of student thinking and determine implications for instructional practices. Wickstrom (2015) also found the teachers questioned their previously held beliefs about students' ability levels, noticed more advanced levels than they had expected, and adapted instruction to fit the more advanced strategies demonstrated by students. The three case-study teachers came to describe students' reasoning as a continuum. At the close of their work with the researcher, they explained how it was important to understand student thinking instead of grading based on correctness. Having time to think through lessons, plan instructional tasks, and discuss students' thinking with other teachers was something they reported as valuable.

Challenges in Implementation. Teachers reported challenges they faced as they tried to implement LT research into practice. First, it was often difficult to use the LT to coordinate wide-ranging strategies or to categorize students' thinking. Although teachers were open to posing tasks and exploring students' thinking, it took sustained effort for them to keep track of students' thinking over time and determine how to shape instruction to fit such thinking. The teachers said it was [too] difficult to consider all of the students in their classroom at the same time and respond to their instructional needs. In addition, they said that it was challenging to allow time for students to understand a measurement concept in adequate detail. Second, we have found that language in the LT can sometimes be intimidating, especially from the teachers' perspective. Terminology used by researchers, such as *pre-area quantity recognizer* or *area simple comparer* were not easily remembered and understood by teachers. The teachers felt more comfortable discussing students' thinking in their words.

Lastly, as described earlier, many teachers described the need for more examples of mathematical tasks related to the LT. They argued that more tasks, with possible student responses, would be helpful in guiding their teaching and making this research easier to share. This call for tasks and notes about possible responses drove the design and production of our book of tasks for teaching measurement in relation to the LTs (Barrett, Cullen, et al., 2017).

Looking across our workshops between 2011 and 2017, later cohorts of teachers became more comfortable identifying and discussing conceptual aspects of students' actions on measurement tasks. In addition, teachers commented that the combined support of PD facilitators and their peer teachers helped them integrate research ideas into practice. Teachers also noted the difficulty of changing or improving tasks. Task design was not always easy because teachers' textbook series and their prior professional learning had rarely focused on conceptual aspects of geometric measurement. It is important to continue to research and publish measurement tasks that teachers can use in their classrooms. In addition, we believe that teacher learning is generative in that coordinating and categorizing students' thinking may become easier as teachers experience wider ranges of tasks and have time to practice using those tasks to predict and check student thinking. As resources emerge and as teachers enact rich measurement tasks multiple times, they may become more comfortable with the content and more attuned to addressing subtleties in students' reasoning.

DESIGNERS LEARNING THROUGH PD IMPLEMENTATION

Using an LT to inform instruction is multifaceted and involves different, interconnected tasks of teaching. Teachers need to be able to write open-ended tasks, observe and record students' thinking, respond appropriately to students, and use what they know about students' mathematical thinking to design and implement subsequent tasks in future lessons. Regardless of how long a teacher has taught, he needs practice with all of these skills in order to be effective in the classroom. In this section, we reflect on multiple rounds of PD and discuss our realizations as designers, changes in the PD over time, and changes in the representations of the LT.

Major Realization of the Designers

As designers, we learned that teachers need pedagogical and organizational tools to productively respond to what they notice during classroom instruction and student interviews. Throughout all of our professional development workshops, we provided teachers with LTs as a tool for them to develop methods for understanding student thinking at a deep mathematical level. Rather than having teachers focus on whether or not a student got a correct answer, we had teachers identify specific LT levels. We discussed what each LT level means, what indicators might flag a given level, and how to create, modify, or find tasks that are appropriate. Conversations during the professional development focused on how to use the LT to respond to students' solution strategies, guide student thinking during individual, small-group, and whole-class discussions, and move students' thinking forward. Thus, LTs became a tool for teachers to plan appropriate lessons for their students, evaluate and guide student thinking during the lesson, and plan future lessons.

We worked consistently to support the professionalism of teaching. There is a reflexive relationship between a professional development facilitator and a teacher/participant of a professional development workshop. We saw teachers as collaborators, encouraging them to bring their own experiences to the work. They were co-researchers in the planning, implementation, and evaluation process of a lesson. For example, we involved half the teachers from one summer cohort to cooperate with us in leading the next cohort.

In the lesson-study tradition, within workshops and lesson observations, our discussions focused on the tasks within the lesson, the ways in which students responded to the lesson, and how to revise tasks for the next time the lesson is taught, rather than discussing the actions of the teacher. Allowing teachers to become participants and observers in lesson discussions and lesson-study meetings was powerful in helping teachers see and experience what we as researchers were trying to convey throughout the entire professional development.

Changes in PD Design

Reflecting on the professional development workshop after the first year (2011), we realized that providing LTs only as tools was not enough for teachers to develop the skills necessary to be effective classroom teachers. Though they could classify student thinking in terms of an LT level and could recognize what good questioning techniques look like, the teachers still struggled with guiding student thinking, planning appropriate tasks, and leading classroom discussions themselves. Thus, for the second year of the professional development, we decided to introduce the book *5 Practices for Orchestrating Productive Mathematics Discussion* (Smith & Stein, 2011) as an additional resource to help teachers plan lessons to address student thinking, which was consistent with our formative assessment goal of the professional development. This book allowed us to focus on general classroom practices such as anticipating student thinking, asking questions in order not to lose the integrity of a task/lesson, and developing systematic ways for having students share responses. Using the book focused on discussion, in conjunction with the research accounts of student thinking in the LTs, helped teachers develop skills for supporting a range of thinking levels in their class.

Another change we made was to emphasize the interaction between the LT tools and the mathematical goals for the lessons. We needed better ways to bridge the gap between what research has found and what trajectories mean for classroom teaching. We eventually cooperated with teachers to create lessons where the mathematical goal(s) of the lesson directly related to topics and levels found in the LTs.

We also changed how and when we introduced LTs to teachers during the professional development. We wanted teachers to engage in the mathematical ideas of measurement and assessment of students' knowledge before they designed instruction. Thus, for the summer 2011 cohort, we provided teachers with LTs right away, discussed what an LT is, and how to use LTs to classify student thinking. Next, we presented problems to motivate varying levels of thinking. Teachers were asked to consider how their students may solve the problems and role-play how they would respond if they were a student at a specific trajectory level. Then we showed video clips of children solving the same problem and asked teachers to classify student thinking based on the trajectory. In doing this, teachers did not always attend to students' mathematical thinking in ways that were useful for discussion or design of tasks; the teachers often struggled to identify a level to fit the student actions or the wording to describe the actions. This led us to redesign the workshop the next time.

Beginning with the next cohort, in summer 2012, we introduced the exact descriptions of the LT levels later in the workshop. We started by having teachers engage in the mathematical activities themselves, then provided student work samples (either written or video), and asked teachers to group the students in categories. Which student(s) had more sophisticated ways of reasoning mathematically? Why? After this discussion, the LT was introduced and used as a tool for naming and classifying student thinking. This helped convey the importance of using LTs as rubrics for categorizing student thinking.

During the original 2011 workshop sequence, we had the teachers design and choose the focus of a public lesson for the fall lesson study. As PD facilitators, we provided support and feedback without substantively changing their plans. However, we learned the teachers tended to emphasize classroom management rather than focusing on conceptual measurement development as they designed the lessons that first time. Thus, we decided to stay more closely involved in the lesson-design work for lesson-study work beginning in 2012. In the second summer workshop, we increased the level of researcher involvement in the design of classroom lessons and placed more emphasis on the importance of studying students' reasoning about measurement within the lesson study.

Changes in Representations of the LT

The LT document has been revisited and refined based on research surrounding students' mathematical reasoning (Barrett, Clements, & Sarama, 2017). When translating our research to teachers, we realized that teachers benefit from working with sample tasks at each level. We realized teachers must observe, study, and categorize many instances of students' thinking just as we must do so as researchers. Teachers benefitted from shared planning and conversation while working from level to level with examples. Wickstrom reports subsequent related work with elementary teachers using ideas from LTs on measurement (Wickstrom & Jurczak, 2016; Wickstrom et al., 2015). In helping the teachers witness students' actions and understanding from the LT, Wickstrom encouraged them to work through the task and imagine the task from the student viewpoint. Similarly, we have used sample lessons from the book *A Pleasure to Measure* (Barrett, Cullen, et al., 2017) to help teachers grasp a conceptual view of measurement for length, area, and volume. The most productive conversations were organized around repeated classroom experimentation with the lessons, providing teachers ways to watch their students grapple with measurement from a new role, that of experimenter or scientist, and not merely as a technician. The 22 teachers in the 2016 and 2017 cohorts reported that working on a lesson with a collaborator, a coach, has given them ways of watching for conceptual thinking. These opportunities led them to envision new ways to discuss mathematical aspects of measurement with their students.

In our professional development work we have come to see ourselves working as *teacher researchers* (Cochran-Smith & Lytle, 1993); we encourage teachers to join in the research process within their own classrooms. By making sense of students' thinking for themselves, teachers construct understanding of the LT in their own ways, often in alignment with the ways in which others who are also researchers consider students' thinking. We believe there is a freedom and a professional benefit in this perspective: The teachers consult the LT but also learn to question broader content, tools, and practices in their teaching. In closing, our work with teachers has helped show that teachers benefit from multiple support structures when integrating research on students' thinking into practice. Support in developing and planning lessons, support from other practitioners and researchers, and support in understanding mathematical content have all been critical for implementing successful PD.

NOTE

This material is based on work supported by the National Science Foundation under Grant No. (DRL 0732217 and DRL 1222944). Any opinions, findings, and conclusions or recommendations expressed in this material are those of the authors and do not necessarily reflect the views of the National Science Foundation. We also acknowledge funding support for this work from the Illinois State Board of Education as a Math Science Partnership project.

REFERENCES

Barrett, J. E., Clements, D. H., & Sarama, J. (2017). Children's measurement: A longitudinal study of children's knowledge and learning of length, area, and volume. *Journal for Research in Mathematics Education* Monograph Series (Vol. 16). Reston, VA.

Barrett, J. E., Cullen, C. J., Behnke, D., & Klanderman, D. (2017). *A Pleasure to Measure! Tasks for Teaching Measurement in the Elementary Grades*. Reston, VA: National Council of Teachers of Mathematics.

Barrett, J. E., Sarama, J., Clements, D. H., Cullen, C. J., McCool, J., Witkowski, C., & Klanderman, D. (2012). Children's abstraction of iterative units to measure linear space: A trajectory. *Mathematical Thinking and Learning, 14*(1), 28–54.

Barrett, J. E., Sarama, J., Clements, D. H., Cullen, C. J., Rumsey, C., Miller, A. L., & Klanderman, D. (2011). Children's unit concepts in measurement: A teaching experiment spanning grades 2 through 5. *ZDM: the International Journal on Mathematics Education, 43*(5), 637–650. doi:10.1007/s11858-011-0368-8

Behr, M. J., Khoury, H. A., Harel, G., Post, T., & Lesh, R. (1997). Conceptual units analysis of pre-service elementary school teachers: Strategies on a rational-number-as-operator task. *Journal for Research in Mathematics Education, 28*, 48–69.

Clements, D. H., & Sarama, J. (2004). Hypothetical Learning Trajectories. *Mathematical Thinking and Learning, 6*(2), 81–90.

Clements, D. H., & Sarama, J. (2009). *Learning and teaching early math: The learning trajectories approach.* New York, NY: Routledge.

Clements, D. H., Sarama, J., Spitler, M. E., Lange, A., & Wolfe, C. B. (2011). Mathematics learned by young children in an intervention based on learning trajectories: A large-scale cluster randomized trial. *Journal for Research in Mathematics Education, 42*(2), 127–166.

Cobb, P., Wood, T., Yackel, E., Nichols, J., Wheatley, G., Tragatti, B., & Pearlwitz, M. (1991). Assessment of a problem-centered second-grade mathematics project. *Journal for Research in Mathematics Education, 22*, 3–29.

Cochran-Smith, M., & Lytle, S. L. (1993). *Inside/outside: Teacher research and knowledge.* New York, NY: Teachers College Press.

Cuneo, D. O. (1980). A general strategy for quantity judgments: The height + width rule. *Child Development, 51*(1), 299–301.

Fennema, E., Carpenter, T. P., Franke, M. L., Levi, L., Jacobs, V. R., & Empson, S. B. (1996). A longitudinal study of learning to use children's thinking in mathematics instruction. *Journal for Research in Mathematics Education, 27*(4), 403–434.

Fernandez, C. (2005). Lesson study: A means for elementary teachers to develop the knowledge of mathematics needed for reform-minded teaching? *Mathematical Thinking & Learning: An International Journal, 7*(4), 265–289.

Ginsburg, H. P. (2009). The challenge of formative assessment in mathematics education: Children's minds, teachers' minds. *Human Development, 52*, 109–128.

Jacobs, V. R., Lamb, C. E., & Philipp, R. A. (2010). Professional noticing of children's mathematical thinking. *Journal for Research in Mathematics Education, 41*(2), 169–202.

Lobato, J., & Walters, C. D. (2017). A taxonomy of approaches to learning trajectories and progressions. In J. Cai (Ed.), *Compendium for research in mathematics education* (pp. 74–101). Reston, VA: National Council of Teachers of Mathematics.

McCool, J. (2009). *Measurement learning trajectories: A tool for professional development* (Doctoral dissertation). Illinois State University, Normal, IL.

Mullet, E., & Paques, P. (1991). The height + width = area of a rectangle rule in five-year-olds: Effects of stimulus distribution and graduation of the response scale. *Journal of Experimental Child Psychology, 52*(3), 336–343.

Ramaprasad, A. (1983). On the definition of feedback. *Behavioural Science, 28*(1), 4–13.

Rulence-Paques, P., & Mullet, E. (1998). Area judgment from width and height information: The case of the rectangle. *Journal of Experimental Child Psychology, 69*(1), 22–48.

Schifter, D., Bastable, V., & Russell, S. J. (2002). *Measuring space in one, two and three dimensions*. Parsippany, NJ: Pearson Learning Group.

Silver, E. A., & Lunsford, C. (2017). Linking research and practice in mathematics education: Perspectives and pathways. In J. Cai (Ed.), *Compendium for research in mathematics education* (pp. 28–47). Reston, VA: National Council of Teachers of Mathematics.

Smith, J. P., Males, L. M., & Gonulates, F. (2016). Conceptual limitations in curricular presentations of area measurement: One nation's challenges. *Mathematical Thinking and Learning, 18*(4), 239–270. doi:10.1080/10986065.2016.1219930

Smith, M. S., & Stein, M. K. (2011). *5 Practices for orchestrating productive mathematics discussions*. Reston, VA: National Council of Teachers of Mathematics.

Takahashi, A., & McDougal, T. (2018). Collaborative lesson research (CLR). In M. Quaresma, C. Winsløw, S. Clivaz, J. da Ponte, A. Ní Shúilleabháin, & A. Takahashi (Eds.), *Mathematics lesson study around the world* (pp. 143–152). Cham, Switzerland: Springer.

Thanheiser, E., Olanoff, D., Hillen, A., Feldman, Z., Tobias, J. M., & Welder, R. M. (2016). Reflective analysis as a tool for task redesign: The case of prospective elementary teachers solving and posing fraction comparison problems. *Journal of Mathematics Teacher Education, 19*(2), 123–148. doi:10.1007/s10857-015-9334-7

Weber, E., & Lockwood, E. (2014). The duality between ways of thinking and ways of understanding: Implications for learning trajectories in mathematics education. *The Journal of Mathematical Behavior, 35*, 44–57. doi:https://doi.org/10.1016/j.jmathb.2014.05.002

Wickstrom, M. H. (2014). An examination of teachers' perceptions and implementation of learning trajectory based professional development (Doctoral dissertation). Illinois State University, Normal, IL.

Wickstrom, M. H. (2015). Challenging a teacher's perceptions of mathematical smartness through reflections on students' thinking. *Equity & Excellence in Education, 48*(4), 589–605.

Wickstrom, M. H., Baek, J., Barrett, J. E., Tobias, J. M., & Cullen, C. J. (2012, Nov.). *Teachers' noticing of children's understanding of linear measurement*. Paper presented at the 34th annual meeting of the North American Chapter of the International Group for the Psychology of Mathematics Education, Kalamazoo, MI.

Wickstrom, M. H., & Jurczak, L. M. (2016). Inch by inch, we measure. *Teaching Children Mathematics, 22*(8), 468–475.

Wickstrom, M. H., Nelson, J., & Chumbley, J. (2015). Area conceptions sprout on Earth Day. *Teaching Children Mathematics, 21*(4), 466–474.

Wiliam, D. (2007). Keeping learning on track: Classroom assessment and the regulation of learning. In F. K. Lester Jr. (Ed.), *Second handbook of mathematics teaching and learning* (pp. 1053–1098). Greenwich, CT: Information Age Publishing.

Wilson, P. H. (2009). *Teachers' uses of a learning trajectory for equipartitioning* (Doctoral dissertation). North Carolina State University, Raleigh, NC.

CHAPTER 4

The Responsive Teaching in Elementary Mathematics Project

*Victoria R. Jacobs, Susan B. Empson, D'Anna Pynes,
Amy Hewitt, Naomi Jessup, and Gladys Krause*

> The way we question the kids about their [ideas] . . . just opens up this total
> new world of where they are. I think that's been the most eye-opening and
> important thing for me, because now, no matter what it is I am teaching, I
> feel like I am comfortable enough to go in and say, "Tell me what you are
> thinking here." And now . . . they feel comfortable answering—and not like,
> "Oh, what's the right way to tell her? What answer is she looking for?" They
> are getting used to just saying, "Well here was what I was thinking, and this is
> how I did it."

These ideas were shared by a 4th-grade teacher completing her second of
3 years of PD in the Responsive Teaching in Elementary Mathematics
(RTEM) project.[1] The goal for this PD was to help teachers develop mathematics instruction that was responsive to children's ways of reasoning. To
be responsive in this way, teachers must not only value children's thinking but also elicit, make sense of, and build on children's existing ideas.
A fundamental aspect of this work is to regularly ask children about their
mathematical ideas and reasoning, which, as the teacher in the opening
quote expressed, gives teachers access to this "total new world" of children's
thinking.

In this chapter, we share how we explored teaching that is responsive to
children's thinking with teachers of grades 3–5 in the context of teaching and
learning fractions. We begin by sharing our vision of this type of responsive
teaching and identifying knowledge and instructional practices needed to enact it. We then describe our study, provide an overview of our PD design
principles, and conclude with two sections about what was learned through
this study—learning by teachers who participated in the PD and learning by
us as PD designers.

VISION OF RESPONSIVE TEACHING

Our RTEM project, along with the other projects described in this book, illustrates PD that supports teachers in developing expertise in K–12 mathematics instruction in which children's thinking plays a central role. We talk about this type of teaching as *responsive teaching* and adopt the three characterizing features identified by Richards and Robertson (2016): (a) attending to the substance of children's ideas, (b) recognizing the important mathematical connections within those ideas, and (c) taking up and pursuing those ideas. This vision of instruction connects to a large body of research and policy documents that outline the details of children's thinking in specific mathematical content areas and demonstrate the benefits of mathematics instruction in which children's thinking plays a central role (see, e.g., Cai, 2017; National Council of Teachers of Mathematics, 2014; National Research Council, 2001).

Despite strong evidence of the importance of responsive teaching, achieving this vision has proven challenging. Responsive teaching requires complex, in-the-moment expertise in addition to the multiple responsibilities typically associated with any type of teaching. Rather than follow scripted teaching moves identified in advance of a lesson, responsive teachers need to notice the details of children's ideas that emerge during a lesson and use these ideas—in the midst of instruction—to make decisions about what to pursue and how to pursue it (Jacobs & Empson, 2016).

Before describing how we focused on helping teachers develop this in-the-moment expertise in our PD, we acknowledge that we are foregrounding only one of many types of responsiveness. In this chapter, we use the term *responsive teaching* to refer to teaching that is responsive to children's mathematical thinking, which is critical if children are to learn mathematics with understanding. However, there are other important ways in which teachers need to be responsive to children. In particular, we note the importance of culturally responsive teaching, which highlights the need for teachers to be responsive not only to children's thinking but also to children's identities that reflect their cultural, linguistic, and community-based resources (see e.g., Gay, 2002; Ladson-Billings, 1995). We view these two forms of responsiveness as working in tandem—informing and mutually enhancing each other (Turner et al., 2016)—and also suggest that supporting teachers in exploring children's mathematical thinking can provide an entry point for teachers to get to know children not only mathematically but also more holistically (Battey & Chan, 2010).

SUPPORTING THE DEVELOPMENT OF EXPERTISE IN RESPONSIVE TEACHING

To support the development of the in-the-moment expertise needed for teaching that is responsive to children's thinking, we introduced teachers to multiple *frameworks*, which are structures in which related ideas are organized to facilitate their understanding and use. We shared two types of frameworks that encapsulated research findings—one focused on *children's thinking* and the other focused on *instructional practices*—and we engaged teachers in integrating these frameworks into their teaching. We believe that using only one of these types of frameworks is insufficient for helping teachers develop expertise in responsive teaching, and throughout the chapter, we highlight the power of pairing children's-thinking frameworks with instructional-practices frameworks.

Frameworks of Children's Thinking

Teaching responsively on the basis of children's thinking is not possible without knowledge of children's thinking. Our children's-thinking frameworks are connected to the longstanding research and PD project Cognitively Guided Instruction (CGI), which has a strong history of documented benefits for children and teachers (see e.g., Carpenter, Fennema, Peterson, Chiang, & Loef, 1989; Fennema et al., 1996; Jacobs, Franke, Carpenter, Levi, & Battey, 2007). CGI involves both research-based knowledge of how *children* think about mathematics (vs. how *adults* think about mathematics) and a strengths-based philosophy that connects this body of knowledge with the idea that instruction should elicit and build on children's ideas (vs. focusing on the ideas they are lacking). In CGI PD, the emphasis is on supporting teachers while they work to enhance their instructional decisionmaking linked to children's thinking in the context of their own instruction. Teachers' knowledge of mathematics is addressed by foregrounding children's thinking and highlighting the mathematical content in children's strategies, because children's mathematical thinking and mathematical content are considered to be intertwined.

CGI researchers have explored instruction that builds on children's thinking about whole-number concepts and operations (Carpenter, Fennema, Franke, Levi, & Empson, 2015), early number concepts (Carpenter, Franke, Johnson, Turrou, & Wager, 2016), early algebra (Carpenter, Franke, & Levi, 2003), and fractions (Empson & Levi, 2011). In the RTEM project, we contribute to this line of work with our focus on instruction that builds on children's thinking about fractions. Specifically, we drew on research presented in the Empson and Levi (2011) book *Extending Children's Mathematics: Fractions and Decimals* to share two types of children's-thinking frameworks to help teachers support children in understanding fractions. First, we shared a *problem-type framework* in which categories of story problems (problem types) are distinguished based on both children's views of problem difficulty and how children initially make sense of and solve problems. Second, we shared a *strategy framework* that includes, for each problem type, the range of children's typical strategies in an order that reflects increasing levels of understanding of fractions. More information about the problem-type and strategy frameworks for fractions can be found in Empson and Levi (2011), but we provide a small illustration of the frameworks here.

Consider how children might distinguish between the following two division problems in terms of problem difficulty and solution strategy.

- There are 3 bars of clay and each child needs ¾ of a bar of clay to make a clay animal. How many children can make clay animals?
- There are 4 children sharing 3 bars of clay to make clay animals. How much clay can each child have if everyone gets the same amount?

These two division problems are distinguished in the *problem-type framework* because children distinguish between them in their strategies and how they view their difficulty, and these distinctions are important for instruction. Even though these problems deal with the same quantities, children initially find the second problem to be simpler than the first problem because no fraction words or notation are included in the problem statement, so children can draw on their whole-number knowledge to begin solving the problem. Specifically, they can draw the three bars of clay, partition them into pieces, and distribute pieces to the four children. They may not use all of the bars of clay or be able to formally name the amount of clay that each child receives, but the problem is still accessible, in part because fraction words and notation are needed only for the final answer, not the problem solving. In contrast, the first problem is initially more challenging because the fraction ¾ is part of the problem statement and therefore, to even begin to solve the problem, children need to be able to make sense of the fraction ¾, whether it is presented in words or notation. According to the problem-type framework, the first problem would be identified as *multiple groups measurement division* and the second problem as *multiple groups partitive division* (or *equal sharing*). These problem-type names are not meant to be shared with children but are instead specialized vocabulary for teachers to help them reflect on and discuss how children typically engage with these division problems differently.

In the *strategy framework*, children's typical strategies that reflect various levels of understanding of fractions are distinguished, and Figure 4.1 provides sample strategies for the two division problems. For example, the strategy Izaiah used to solve the first problem is identified as a *direct-modeling* strategy in the strategy framework. He drew circles to represent the three bars of clay, partitioned each into fourths, and gave three-fourths of the first bar to one child, three-fourths of the second bar to a second child, and three-fourths of the third bar to a third child. He then distributed the final three-fourths to a fourth child by collecting the leftover one-fourth from each of the three bars and concluded that four children could make clay animals. In this strategy, Izaiah directly modeled the problem situation because he explicitly represented every quantity, including the fractional parts and the wholes. In contrast, Jimena did not need to represent the wholes or the relationship between the fractional parts and the wholes. She instead represented the fractional part—the amount of clay needed for each child—as a numerical abstraction (¾) and operated on it repeatedly. Specifically, Jimena counted up by three-fourths and recorded each count symbolically, as a running total. She stopped counting when she reached three because, at that point, she had used all three bars of clay. She then determined her answer of four children by counting the number of times she had counted (added) three fourths. In the strategy framework, Jimena's strategy is identified as a *counting/adding* strategy, which reflects a more

Figure 4.1. Frameworks of Children's Thinking

		There are 3 bars of clay and each child needs ¾ of a bar of clay to make a clay animal. How many children can make clay animals?	*There are 4 children sharing 3 bars of clay to make clay animals. How much clay can each child have if everyone gets the same amount?*
Problem-Type Framework		Multiple Groups Measurement Division	Multiple Groups Partitive Division (Equal Sharing)
Strategy Framework	*Strategies reflecting early understandings of fractions*	Direct-Modeling Strategy Figure A Izaiah	Direct-Modeling Strategy (Non-Anticipatory) Figure B Lily
	Strategies reflecting more advanced understandings of fractions	Counting/Adding Strategy Figure C Jimena	Direct-Modeling Strategy (Emergent Anticipatory) Figure D Anthony

advanced level of understanding of fractions than is reflected in *direct-modeling* strategies. Similar to the problem-type names, strategy names are not meant to be shared with children but instead are specialized vocabulary for teachers to facilitate their learning in PD and their use of these ideas when reflecting on their own practices.

Design Features of Our Children's-Thinking Frameworks.

Design Features of Our Children's-Thinking Frameworks. We close our discussion of children's-thinking frameworks by clarifying the design features that underlie their construction and intended use. Like the other authors of this book, we value children's thinking as foundational for instruction and believe that instruction can be enhanced when teachers are given access to research-based knowledge about how children's thinking develops over time. However, in each project depicted in the book, this research-based knowledge is organized and used differently, and in this section, we describe our approach.

Our frameworks are designed to support teachers' responsiveness to children's thinking by helping them organize and use what they see and hear when children are solving problems during instruction. To facilitate this in-the-moment use of our frameworks in the fast-paced environment of the classroom, we purposefully designed the frameworks to identify only a small number of broad categories. These broad categories necessarily have more variability within them than categories identified by other approaches that organize children's thinking in ways that are intended to be more exhaustive. For teachers to make sense of this variability, they need to take ownership of the frameworks and customize the broad categories for themselves as they engage with their students' ideas during instruction. This customization of the frameworks by teachers is a purposeful part of our framework design to (a) counteract inclinations to use the framework categories to prescribe instruction and (b) support a vision of responsive teaching, which, by definition, does not look the same in every situation because teachers need to respond to the specific children in their classrooms. We share one example of teachers' customization to give readers a sense of what is possible.

This example of a 4th-grade teacher's customization of the strategy framework showcases how teachers do not feel bound by the small number of broad categories and instead sometimes choose to create new categories based on what they see and hear from their students. In this example, the teacher identified a new strategy category when describing her process for planning a whole-class discussion. Specifically, after her students had an opportunity to solve a fraction story problem, she collected and reviewed the written work to select a few strategies to showcase in a whole-class discussion, often called a *sharing session*. To facilitate her strategy selection, she began by sorting her students' written work into piles, many of which corresponded to distinctions in our strategy framework. For instance, she distinguished *direct-modeling* strategies (in which children often use pictures to explicitly represent problem situations, including all of the quantities) from strategies in which children no longer need to create pictorial models and thus more typically solve problems using numerical representations. However, this teacher also felt that—to capture the understandings reflected in her students' strategies—an additional distinction was useful, and she created a new pile to represent this new strategy category. Strategies in this category appeared to be in transition between two broad categories in the framework. She called the students using strategies in this new category "semi-modelers" and described them as individuals who "use a little modeling and some numbers, but they're not confident with just going cold-turkey without a model." Grouping the semi-modelers' strategies was a distinction that this teacher found to be helpful for her decisionmaking with this particular group of students (but may not be helpful for other teachers with other students in other instructional contexts). Our emphasis on a small number of broad categories in the design of the strategy framework facilitated this type of customization in which attention to the details of her own students' strategies allowed this teacher to take ownership of the framework.

In summary, when we engage teachers with our frameworks, our focus is less about helping them learn the names of categories of problems and strategies and more about helping them experience the distinctions as they work with children to develop a deep understanding of the research-based knowledge of children's thinking. Further, as teachers gain expertise in decisionmaking in which children's thinking is central, they assume ownership of and customize the frameworks by drawing on their understanding of their own instructional contexts. Our emphasis on customization helps to explain why we conceptualize our organizational structures for the research-based knowledge of children's thinking as *frameworks* rather than *learning trajectories* (or *learning progressions*).

Our use of frameworks reflects not only our strong historical ties to CGI (Carpenter et al., 2015)—which has used frameworks for the past 30 years—but also our belief that the metaphor of a framework better captures our priorities. In contrast to the metaphor of a trajectory, which can connote a sequenced path for instruction (Empson, 2011), we choose the metaphor of a framework—a supporting structure that is multidimensional and broad rather than exhaustive in nature—which captures our design choice to use a small number of broad categories inviting teachers' flexible use and customization with specific children and instructional contexts. We further reinforce our emphasis on teachers' *use* of children's-thinking frameworks by pairing them with instructional-practices frameworks. This purposeful pairing reflects our view that learning about children's-thinking frameworks is an integral part of gaining expertise in the instructional practices that underlie responsive teaching, and not simply an end in itself. We turn next to these instructional-practices frameworks.

Frameworks of Instructional Practices

Like all teaching, responsive teaching involves a variety of instructional practices. In our PD, we shared research-based frameworks for two practices that are core to responsive teaching and highlight the central role that children's thinking plays in this type of teaching: *noticing children's mathematical thinking* and *questioning to build on children's mathematical thinking*. We conceptualized both of these practices as *knowledge intensive* in that teachers must use knowledge of children's mathematical thinking to enact the practices. By engaging teachers with frameworks for both instructional practices and children's thinking, we underscore the idea that although gaining knowledge about children's thinking is critical, teachers need more than this knowledge to enact responsive teaching. Likewise, although focusing on instructional practices is critical, teachers need more than these practices to enact responsive teaching.

Noticing Framework. The noticing framework, which is focused on noticing children's mathematical thinking, is the first of the instructional-practices frameworks used in our PD. When children share their ideas in comments, questions, actions, or written work, teachers need to—in the moment—identify and make sense of the important mathematical details prior to responding. These seemingly simple, but actually complex, encounters occur over and over during a lesson, and they require this hidden instructional practice that we call *noticing*.

Our noticing framework is based on prior work on noticing children's mathematical thinking (Jacobs, Lamb, & Philipp, 2010), which identified three interrelated component skills that occur quickly and almost simultaneously during instruction. In our noticing framework, these three categories of skills are made explicit:

- *attending* to the details in children's strategies
- *interpreting* children's understandings reflected in their strategies
- *deciding how to respond* on the basis of children's understandings

Note that this final skill—*deciding how to respond*—refers to teachers' *intended* responding because the practice of noticing occurs before teachers actually respond. Teachers' *actual* (enacted) responses may not always exactly match their intentions, but unless teachers are intending to respond on the basis of children's understandings, they are unlikely to do so, and thus we have found intended responding to be a productive focus for PD.

Consider the example of Lily's strategy for the equal-sharing problem in Figure 4.1. *Attending* to the details of her strategy requires more than recognizing that her answer of "2 peices" is imprecise, because much of her strategy is valid. Specifically, she partitioned two bars of clay into halves and distributed one-half bar to each child. She also partitioned the last bar of clay into fourths and distributed one-fourth bar to each child. Thus, Lily distributed the same amount to each child, and her final answer of "2 peices" reflected this valid partitioning and distribution even though she did not use conventional fraction words or notation. *Interpreting* Lily's understandings reflected in these strategy details requires a focus on what she does (vs. does not) understand. Her strategy revealed an understanding that problems such as this one are about partitioning, involve equal partitions, require all the items to be shared completely, and necessitate that everyone receive the same amount. Finally, *deciding how to respond* on the basis of Lily's understandings requires selection among multiple possible next steps that could be productive given that no single step or type of step is best. Some possible productive next steps include asking Lily about how she chose to partition the items in the ways that she did and how she was thinking about the relative size of the "two peices." These sample questions reflect only a few of the possible next steps but notably build on Lily's ideas and reasoning (vs. simply highlighting her errors or incomplete work that needs to be adjusted).

In summary, we used the noticing framework, with its three component skills, to help teachers recognize and explore the complexity of noticing children's mathematical thinking during instruction. After teachers have noticed children's thinking, including identifying their intended responses, they still must carry out the responses. We turn next to those responses, which are often in the form of questions.

Questioning Framework. The questioning framework, which is focused on questioning to build on children's mathematical thinking, is the second of the instructional-practices frameworks used in our PD. In responsive teaching, teachers' questions are formulated by taking into account the details of children's thinking that emerge in the lesson rather than on the basis of predetermined lesson scripts or questioning routines. To support this type of questioning, we shared a questioning framework that provided categories of questioning purposes rather than lists of specific questions. Question lists can be problematic because no question is appropriate in all situations for all children. However, teachers do need some support because coordinating information about the details of children's thinking and formulating questions *in the moment* is challenging to enact. Categories of questioning purposes can support teachers by making questioning seem more manageable while also encouraging the formulation of specific questions based on what is appropriate for specific children at that moment.

Our questioning framework is based on prior work (Jacobs & Ambrose, 2008; Jacobs & Empson, 2016) and makes explicit five categories of questioning purposes:

- Ensuring that children are making sense of story problems
- Exploring details of children's existing strategies
- Encouraging children to consider other strategies
- Connecting children's thinking to symbolic notation
- Posing a related problem linked to what children understand

These categories of questioning purposes are not intended as a checklist for teachers to use in every situation. Instead, the categories are designed to serve as a toolbox from which teachers can draw, depending on the situation. For example, in response to Lily's strategy in Figure 4.1, teachers might pose questions from the category of *exploring details of children's existing strategies,* such as the intended questions suggested in the earlier section on noticing, which inquired about Lily's partitioning and the relative sizes of the resulting quantities. Questions related to this category are particularly helpful in encouraging children to explain or justify specific problem-solving steps that are mathematically important. Another potentially helpful questioning category for Lily is *posing a related problem linked to what children understand.* For instance, teachers might pose a problem to Lily like the following in which combining different-sized pieces would be less likely:

There are 2 children sharing 7 bars of clay to make clay animals. How much clay can each child have if everyone gets the same amount?
For this new problem, many children like Lily would either partition all seven bars in half or distribute six whole bars of clay (three per child) and then partition the final bar in half. With either of these strategies, Lily's work would reveal whether she was comfortable using fraction names or notation in a less complex situation in which she did not need to combine different-sized pieces.

In contrast, teachers may be less likely to ask Lily questions related to the other categories of questioning purposes, such as *ensuring that children are making sense of story problems.* Questions related to this category (e.g., "Can you tell me in your own words what the problem is asking?") can be particularly helpful in situations when children are struggling to unpack the story context or make sense of the mathematical question. However, through her valid strategy, Lily has already shown that she has made sense of the problem and thus questioning for this purpose may be less helpful.

Collectively, the frameworks of children's thinking and instructional practices have been central to our efforts to help teachers develop expertise in responsive teaching. In the next section, we describe the guiding principles for the design of our PD, including how we supported teachers to take up and use these frameworks.

RTEM: A DESIGN-BASED PD STUDY

RTEM is a multiyear design-based PD study in which our main goals are to support and characterize the development of teaching that is responsive to children's fraction thinking in grades 3–5. In a design-based study such as ours, researchers repeat (or iterate) the PD multiple times, each time incorporating refinements that are informed by the previous iterations (Design-Based Research Collective, 2003).

Our PD consisted of more than 150 hours offered over 3 years, with each year including 4.5 workshop days during the summer and 4 workshop days during the school year (2 consecutive days in the fall and 2 consecutive days in the spring). The researchers did not teach the workshops but instead worked collaboratively with PD facilitators to design and continually refine the activities and materials. In addition, the PD included several school-based activities that were enacted by teachers between workshops and without a PD facilitator present. The overall goal of the PD was to help teachers develop expertise in responsive teaching with fractions, with special emphasis on the practices of noticing children's thinking and questioning to build on children's thinking—both of which are tightly linked to knowledge of children's fraction thinking.

PD Participants

We worked with 92 upper elementary school teachers (82 females and 10 males) who were divided into three cohorts and invited to participate in 3 years of PD. As is typical in designed-based research, we staggered the start of the cohorts' PD so that we could continually make refinements in the PD for subsequent cohorts. When the teachers began the PD, their years of teaching experience ranged from 0 to 34 years (with an average of 10 years), and about one-third had participated in previous CGI PD on children's mathematical thinking with whole numbers.

The teachers were drawn from three districts (involving 11–15 schools per district) in the southern region of the United States. All three district administrations had endorsed the PD and instruction that was responsive to children's mathematical thinking, and these districts were purposely selected because of their varying instructional contexts (Figure 4.2) and histories. District A (24 teachers) and District B (38 teachers) had long histories of supporting their teachers in learning about children's thinking to inform instruction, and multiple district-created resources were available. However, District B was in the midst of shifting priorities given new administration, and less emphasis was being placed on this type of instruction. District C (30 teachers) had only recently begun to embrace teaching that is responsive to children's thinking, and thus resources for teachers were still emerging.

Figure 4.2. District Demographics

		District A	*District B*	*District C*
Students classified as Limited English Proficiency		33%	47%	9%
Students who qualified for free or reduced-cost lunch		61%	71%	40%
Student race and ethnicity classifications	White	48%	36%	68%
	Hispanic	45%	46%	12%
	Black	2%	3%	10%
	Other	5%	15%	10%

Note: These district demographic data reflect the school year in which the highest number of teachers were involved in the RTEM study. Data and demographic classifications were drawn from a state-level database.

PD Design Principles and Activities

We view PD as an opportunity to help teachers learn by reflecting on their existing practices, exploring new ideas, trying new practices, and collaborating with colleagues. As such, our PD engaged teachers in a variety of activities including analyzing children's written work; watching video of individual children solving problems, small-group instruction, and whole-class instruction; working with children; reading about children's thinking and instruction that builds on that thinking; solving mathematics problems using children's strategies; and reviewing and adapting curriculum materials through a lens of children's thinking. The use of these activities with teachers was informed by four design principles, which we unpack and illustrate below: (a) foreground teachers' work with instructional practices, (b) slow the pace of teaching and make instructional practices visible, (c) begin with one-on-one conversations with children, and (d) provide extensive time and experiences across multiple learning spaces.

Principle 1: Foreground Teachers' Work with Instructional Practices. Throughout our PD, we provided opportunities for teachers to learn about and engage with the research-based frameworks of children's fraction thinking and the instructional practices of noticing children's thinking and questioning to build on children's thinking. Knowledge of children's thinking and expertise in the instructional practices are intertwined in that to enact the practices, teachers need to draw on their knowledge of children's thinking. However, we did not view knowledge of children's thinking as a prerequisite for engaging in the practices and instead foregrounded teachers' work with the practices in our PD from the beginning—both in terms of time allotment and activity design. By viewing teachers' work with the practices as an opportunity for developing expertise in both the practices and knowledge of children's thinking, we emphasized knowledge in use (Ball & Cohen, 1999). This approach connects to other national efforts to support the learning of prospective and practicing teachers through a focus on core instructional practices that are generative (Grossman, 2018; Jacobs & Spangler, 2017; McDonald, Kazemi, & Kavanagh, 2013).

Principle 2: Slow the Pace of Teaching and Make Instructional Practices Visible. Our PD was designed to slow the pace of teaching and make visible the instructional practices of noticing children's thinking and questioning to build on children's thinking. In the classroom, these practices occur frequently and rapidly, often without opportunity for reflection. In the PD, we slowed the pace of teaching and made these practices visible in two main ways: using artifacts that depicted children's thinking and providing opportunities for teachers to interact with children in simplified settings.

First, we made extensive use of artifacts of children's thinking (video and written work) to give teachers opportunities to engage in the instructional practices without the in-the-moment pressures of teaching. For example, teachers watched video or examined written work to explore and make sense of the details of children's strategies. We used these artifacts to bring children into the workshops in ways that felt authentic to teachers—the artifacts were generated by real teachers and real children—and these artifacts helped us create shared group experiences that provided opportunities for reflection and discussion. Video could be stopped or replayed, and written work could be examined and re-examined, with the luxury of time and the support of colleagues and the facilitator. Further, in addition to engaging with artifacts that were purposefully selected by us, teachers were sometimes asked to bring written work from their own classrooms so that they could analyze, again with time and support, the thinking of their own students.

Second, we provided teachers with opportunities in the workshops to interact with children in real time, thereby allowing them to engage in the instructional practices of noticing and questioning in simplified environments, and with support. For example, we invited a group of children into the workshop for about 30 minutes and paired teachers so that every two teachers worked with an individual child in a problem-solving interview. The teachers worked together to pose problems and ask follow-up questions to explore the child's thinking. These interviews provided opportunities for teachers to initially engage in the instructional practices with children by working collaboratively and without the added pressures of addressing multiple children's needs simultaneously. In addition to this scaffolding for teacher learning, the inclusion of children in workshops built excitement for exploring children's thinking and helped teachers see the PD ideas in action, thereby underscoring their relevance. These types of activities help to avoid the typical scenario in which teachers are expected to individually take what they have learned in workshops into their complex classrooms without support.

Principle 3: Begin with One-on-One Conversations with Children. Our PD was extensively focused on teachers' one-on-one conversations with children. Sometimes, we had teachers engage in one-on-one conversations linked to artifacts—analyzing one-on-one conversations portrayed in video or analyzing an individual child's sample of written work to generate possible conversations. Other times, teachers engaged in one-on-one conversations when we brought children into the workshops for problem-solving interviews and other activities. We want to be clear that we do not view expertise in one-on-one conversations as the only expertise needed for responsive teaching, but these conversations are powerful starting points. They preserve the complex, interactive nature of teaching while removing the need to also coordinate multiple children's ideas, and thus they provide safe and productive spaces for teachers' learning.

Developing expertise in one-on-one conversations has two additional benefits. First, these experiences help teachers develop an appreciation for the role that *individual* children's thinking plays in responsive teaching in general. Franke and colleagues (2001) have argued that the highest level of expertise is shown by the teacher who goes beyond "the knowledge of thinking of children as a group" and instead "uses what he or she learns about individual students' mathematical thinking to drive instruction" (p. 662). Second, these experiences help teachers develop an appreciation for the learning potential of one-on-one conversations that teachers have with individual children during problem solving. Specifically, when teachers circulate as children are solving problems, they are generally accomplishing many goals, including maintaining classroom management and gathering information about children's strategies and understandings to plan for whole-class sharing sessions (Smith & Stein, 2018) or to plan for instruction the following day. We endorse these goals but also encourage teachers to expand them to consider one-on-one conversations with children as opportunities to elicit, support, and extend those children's thinking. Even though this expanded goal may require new classroom norms that allow teachers to have longer conversations with individual children while circulating, we argue that individual, customized conversations can be powerful for children's learning as well as teachers' learning about children's thinking (Jacobs & Empson, 2016).

Principle 4: Provide Extensive Time and Experiences Across Multiple Learning Spaces. We purposefully designed our PD as a 3-year set of learning experiences because learning to teach responsively is hard work. We are asking teachers to adjust their instructional practices and think about mathematics and mathematics instruction in ways that may be different from how they were taught. Further, even for teachers with considerable expertise, responsive teaching often takes more time than traditional instruction, and thus teachers must find ways to engage in this type of teaching while also meeting district-mandated standards and timelines. Multiple years of learning and support are needed for teachers to gain expertise and extend (or even maintain) this expertise after the PD ends (Franke, Carpenter, Levi, & Fennema, 2001; Jacobs et al., 2010).

In addition to our emphasis on long-term PD, we conceptualized teacher learning as occurring not only in workshops but also outside of workshops in teachers' classrooms and in conversations with colleagues at their schools. Thus, in addition to planning workshops, we orchestrated focused learning experiences outside of workshops where we were not present. For example, prior to each year's fall and spring workshops, we asked teachers to pose problems in their classrooms to explore workshop ideas in relation to their own students. We also created a web-based tool, which we called the Collaborative Inquiry Tool (CIT), to facilitate *face-to-face* conversations among teachers at the same school site. We designed 12 CIT sessions (4 for each of the 3 years of PD) to help teachers work on their noticing expertise with colleagues at their school sites between workshops. Each session incorporated web-based resources and a suggested structure for conversations, but these conversations were intended to be face-to-face, not electronic.

For each 30–45 minute CIT session, two or more colleagues at the same school site convened for a conversation. Prior to the session, teachers posed the same problem to their classes and collected the written work. The CIT conversations were focused on the three component skills of noticing—*attending* to the details in children's strategies, *interpreting* the understandings reflected in those strategies, and *deciding how to respond* on the basis of those understandings. In each session, teachers were initially asked to notice children's thinking in an artifact we selected, which was either video or written work related to the same problem they had posed in their own classrooms. Teachers were then guided in noticing children's thinking in the written work from their students. The CIT included both suggestions for structuring the teachers' conversations around the three component skills of noticing and a written account of our noticing of children's thinking in the artifacts we had selected. However, our noticing was only meant to be a conversation starter, because the main goal for these sessions was for teachers to engage in noticing with their colleagues, in their school sites, and with strategies from their own students. (See Pynes [2018] for more information on the teachers' experiences with the CIT.)

TEACHER LEARNING IN THE RTEM PROJECT

RTEM is a large-scale research project in which extensive data have been collected on teachers' expertise in responsiveness, children's learning, and the design of the PD. Much of the analysis is ongoing, but in this chapter, we focus on self-reported teacher learning in relation to one of our target instructional practices: questioning to build on children's mathematical thinking. We showcase the teachers' perspectives on (a) changes in their instruction related to questioning, (b) the questioning framework as a tool for supporting their learning, and (c) the problem-solving interviews with children as productive spaces for improving their questioning. Data were drawn from 72 focus-group conversations that spanned the three cohorts and the multiple years of PD; for each year they were enrolled in the PD, teachers participated in two focus groups, one during the summer workshop and one during the spring workshop.

Changes in Instruction Related to Questioning

When teachers were asked what they had learned from the PD, "questioning" was one of the most common responses. They reported that their questioning of children's thinking in their classrooms increased, as did their listening to and respect for children's ideas. For example, a teacher described how she used to dismiss children's ideas when they differed from her own ideas, but she now stopped and listened because children "think a lot more logically than we give them credit for." Consistent with this newfound respect for children's thinking came a new purpose for questioning: "Now I'm questioning to figure out their understandings, not necessarily questioning them to get to the right answer."

Questioning children's thinking was also credited for a variety of changes throughout teachers' instruction. For example, teachers reported that questioning children's thinking had led to a decrease in their focus on correct answers only, their tendencies to lead children to those correct answers, and the assumptions they typically made about children's understandings when children's strategies were unclear or did not match the teachers' own understandings. Some teachers also reported that gaining an understanding of children's thinking fundamentally changed the way they planned instruction because they now argued that they could (and should) use children's ideas to determine next instructional steps. (See Figure 4.3 for sample teacher comments that describe these changes in more detail.)

Questioning Framework as a Tool for Teacher Learning

During workshops, teachers spent substantial time engaging with the instructional practice of questioning—with video, written work, and children—and they had opportunities to explore the questioning framework as an instructional tool that could help them elicit and build on children's thinking. Teachers regularly expressed appreciation for the PD emphasis on questioning, which

Figure 4.3. Sample Comments About Instructional Changes Related to Questioning

Less focus on correct answers	It's not about just getting the right answer. I think before I started this training, in my mind, I was always more concerned with what the result was than getting the process. And so this is really neat to go through and focus on how they get that answer and why did they think this way. (Grade 4 teacher)
Less leading	My problem was I always led them, or I wanted to rescue them, you know, cause that's just—that's what a teacher is. You want to rescue your babies. I've had to learn to step back and let them work through it, questioning them but not to lead them. So I feel like that's what this training has really helped me on. (Grade 3 teacher)
Fewer assumptions	You can see what looks like perfect understanding in their work, and without questioning, you think they understand it and they don't. Or you can see something that you cannot even decide for what in the world it is, and ask some questions, and see that they have much deeper understanding, and it is just that they do not know how to write that down. I quit judging what I think they know before I ask. (Grade 5 teacher)
More use of children's thinking in planning instruction	And [the children] are telling me what to do next, what to teach next. When before with [the textbook] it was just go to the lesson and you had to go on. I wasn't sure if they understood or not. . . . That worksheet didn't really tell me what they understood. And now, by asking questions, I know what they are thinking. And they are telling me where I need to go next. (Grade 3 teacher)

they said led to more purposefulness in questioning in their classrooms as well as an increased variety in the questions they posed.

Teachers also expressed appreciation for the questioning framework itself, with one teacher even disclosing her plans to laminate the framework as a tool to assist her while questioning during sharing sessions. In addition to holistic praise for the framework, teachers sometimes cited particular categories of questioning that had made notable differences in their instruction. For example, one teacher highlighted the usefulness of the questioning category of *ensuring that children are making sense of story problem*: "I feel like so often they get lost in the numbers. They forget the details on what these quantities mean, what did they represent. . . . So those types of questions have really helped my kids . . . put themselves back on track." Overall, teachers found the categories of questioning purposes useful for learning about children's thinking and supporting and extending that thinking during instruction.

Problem-Solving Interviews with Children as Spaces for Improving Questioning

Throughout the PD, teachers had multiple opportunities to interview children in workshops, and these experiences were designed to allow teachers to try out and reflect on questioning in real time, but in simplified settings and with support. Teachers almost unanimously endorsed the PD activity of interviewing—in all three years of PD—citing how much they enjoyed and learned from these experiences. As one teacher exclaimed, "What better feedback can you get than [from] the child himself!"

Teachers also articulated specific reasons interviewing in workshops was powerful. Some appreciated how the distraction-free setting supported their learning: "You can really focus on and think about your process, and think about purposeful questioning, and then you get better at it. And you can go back [to your classroom] and . . . because you've done it, you can apply it." Other teachers highlighted how working with children they did not know helped them grow in their questioning. With unfamiliar children, teachers felt a genuine need to ask questions in contrast to tendencies in their own classrooms to skip questioning and instead work from preconceived notions, which can be faulty.

Finally, opportunities to collaborate with colleagues when working with children was one of the most commonly cited reasons teachers appreciated interviewing. Many emphasized the challenging nature of questioning and how partnering provided both encouragement and ideas: "Because you have those moments where you don't know what else to say or you've hit that block and you're like 'Argh!' Then the other person can jump in and they have a question." In addition, the unusualness of these collaborative learning opportunities was recognized because, unlike in their daily routines, teachers were able to see each other in action. For instance, they could hear questions they might not have asked or see conversations taken in directions they might not have gone, and they could learn about their partners' underlying rationales for these questions.

In summary, in our focus groups, teachers vividly described what they had learned about questioning and questioning purposes as well as how they were integrating these ideas into their instruction. They found the questioning framework useful in supporting these changes and particularly appreciated opportunities to use the framework in the simplified setting of interviewing an individual child with a partner.

WHAT WE LEARNED IN THE RTEM PROJECT ABOUT DESIGNING PD

The iterative nature of design-based research enables researchers to progressively refine their design and continually reflect on it. Among the many lessons learned, we highlight one that underscores the power of multiyear PD. Specifically, our work on the RTEM project helped us formalize our ideas about the *importance of engaging teachers in activities that evolve as teachers' expertise evolves over time*. As teachers' noticing and questioning expertise improved, we increased the complexity of our PD activities focused on those instructional practices as well as teachers' responsibilities in the activities. This design gave teachers multiple opportunities to engage in the instructional practices and also helped them to recognize their own growth.

To illustrate the evolution of PD activities for noticing and questioning, we share sample PD activities at two broad time points—earlier and later in teachers' development of expertise (see Figure 4.4 for a summary). *Earlier* and *later* are intentionally broad because the evolution of workshop activities was dependent on multiple factors. Sometimes, our decisions about when to implement different forms of activities were related to the overall chronology of the 3 years of PD in that some forms of activities were deemed too complex for the first year of PD. Other times, these decisions were linked to the extent of teachers' prior engagement with children's thinking in specific content areas, reflecting our view of the instructional practices as knowledge intensive. For example, a particular group of teachers might have moved beyond initial forms of an interviewing activity to more complex forms for equal-sharing problems, but if new content such as children's thinking about decimals was introduced, even in the third year of PD, the interviewing activity might revert to a less complex form. In short, there was not a prescribed timeline in choosing when and how workshop activities evolved. Instead, we considered teachers' evolving expertise and prior experiences with noticing and questioning in the PD overall as well as within particular content areas. In the next sections, we provide a sense of the evolution of our PD activities by sharing sample *earlier* activities and sample *later* activities for noticing and questioning, and for each, we also identify several logistical considerations needed for implementation of the activities.

Evolution of Noticing Activities in RTEM PD

To help teachers learn to notice children's mathematical thinking, we made extensive use of video and written work to engage teachers in a variety of activities that focused on the three component skills of noticing—*attending*, *interpreting*, and *deciding how to respond*. Our selection of artifacts played a critical role in determining the complexity of these activities.

Earlier Noticing Activities. When teachers first worked with the three component skills of the practice of noticing children's mathematical thinking, we generally selected artifacts that included clear and complete strategies that fell neatly within the categories in our strategy framework. An example

Figure 4.4. Sample Evolution of PD Activities in Multiyear RTEM PD

Target Instructional Practices		Sample PD Activities	Evolution of Sample PD Activities
Noticing children's mathematical thinking	*Attending to details in children's strategies*	Describe children's strategies in video or written work	**Using Video and Written Work** *Increased complexity of activities* • Shift from engaging with clear strategies to engaging with ambiguous strategies
	Interpreting children's understandings reflected in strategy details	Describe children's understandings reflected in strategies Sort (and order) strategies according to their increasing levels of understanding of fractions	• Shift from engaging with individual children's strategies to engaging with sets of strategies to consider increasing levels of understanding of fractions *Increased teacher responsibility in activities* • Shift from generating next steps to also refining next steps and linking them to specific instructional goals
	Deciding how to respond on the basis of children's understandings	Generate next instructional steps to build on children's understandings	
	Questioning to build on children's thinking	Interact with one child or more in real time	**Interacting with Children** *Increased complexity of activities* • Shift from a single problem-solving interview to a double interview to interviews linked to small-group sessions *Increased teacher responsibility in activities* • Shift from choosing problems from a small set of problem types and number sets to choosing problems from multiple problem types and number sets (as well as generating number sets) • Shift from focusing on a subset of the questioning framework to the full framework

of such an artifact is Anthony's written work in Figure 4.1, and we use his strategy to illustrate how the component skills of noticing would be addressed in earlier noticing activities.

For the component skill of *attending*, we asked teachers to work together and describe the mathematically important details in children's strategies. For instance, teachers would have an opportunity to articulate that Anthony represented all the bars of clay and partitioned them into fourths. He then distributed the 4 one-fourths from each bar of clay—1 one-fourth to each child—which he recorded using symbolic notation (¼) in the circles (representing children) at the top of his page. He arrived at his answer of ¾ by combining the three one-fourths given to each child. Describing children's strategies fully, especially when strategies are messy or incomplete, can be challenging for teachers who have often had little opportunity to attend closely to strategy details given the fast pace of teaching. Thus, we began with clear examples in which strategy details were most accessible.

For the component skill of *interpreting*, we asked teachers to work together to identify understandings reflected in strategy details and link them to the strategy framework. Therefore, in these earlier noticing activities, we began with strategies that showed strong and clear links to the strategy framework. Anthony's strategy would be clearly identified as *emergent anticipatory direct modeling* in the strategy framework. These strategy details reflected Anthony's need to represent all shares and his ability to coordinate the number of sharers (four) with the number of partitions. In contrast, children using less sophisticated strategies may also represent all the shares, but an understanding of the link between the number of sharers and the number of partitions is often missing.

Finally, for the component skill of *deciding how to respond*, we asked teachers to collaboratively brainstorm about next instructional steps, given a set of strategy details and the understandings they reflected. In these earlier noticing activities, we gave teachers the broad instructional goal of exploring children's thinking when brainstorming next steps and encouraged them to check their impulses to lead children to correct answers or efficient strategies too quickly. To explore Anthony's thinking, teachers might decide to ask him why he partitioned each bar of clay into fourths, or where each child's three "¼s" came from in his drawing of the bars of clay. Our intention was for teachers to come to recognize that multiple productive next steps exist and to see the power in connecting children's understandings with next steps—a connection that may have been in contrast to their typical experiences in which next steps were often driven by pacing guides or textbooks.

Later Noticing Activities. Over the course of the multiyear PD, these noticing activities evolved in two main ways. The first way was that the *complexity of the PD activity increased.* For example, in later noticing activities, rather than always providing clear examples of children's thinking, we changed the nature of the artifacts by including video or written work that depicted strategies that were confusing or incomplete. Teachers had to work harder to make sense of mathematically important details in these strategies and relate them to the strategy framework, and this added complexity provided opportunities to explore the boundaries of student understandings reflected in each framework category. We reiterate that we viewed helping teachers gain familiarity with the framework as more important than always correctly categorizing a particular strategy, because the ultimate goal was to help teachers take ownership of the frameworks and use them as customizable tools.

In addition to adding complexity by changing the nature of the artifacts, we expanded the number of artifacts. In later noticing activities, rather than asking teachers to notice children's thinking in a single strategy, we sometimes presented teachers with sets of strategies to explore. These sets were particularly useful in helping teachers order strategies to think about increasing levels of understanding of fractions, as linked to the strategy framework. However, regularly working with large sets of strategies could have been overwhelming earlier in the PD when teachers were first learning to notice children's thinking in strategies.

The second way that the noticing activities evolved was that the *teachers' responsibilities increased.* For example, we initially asked teachers to generate next instructional steps for the broad goal of exploring children's thinking, whereas in later activities we gave teachers more specific instructional goals (e.g., explore children's thinking in relation to equivalence or notating strategies) or asked them to articulate their own specific goals. We view generating next steps that are connected with specific instructional goals as more complex than generating next steps to broadly explore children's thinking because teachers' tendencies to impose their own ways of reasoning are generally greater when they feel pressure to reach a specific goal, especially when children's ways of reasoning seem far removed from that goal.

In addition, in later noticing activities, we sometimes encouraged teachers to not only generate next steps but also revisit and refine their own and others' next steps. For instance, pairs of teachers generated possible follow-up questions for a child on the basis of his or her written work and a particular instructional goal. Pairs then shared their ideas so that the rest of the teachers in the workshop could consider the questions generated and suggest alternative wording or propose additional questions.

Logistical Considerations for Noticing Activities. Locating and selecting artifacts to use in PD activities is challenging, and we spent a good deal of time collecting artifacts. Video artifacts come in multiple forms, such as (a) one-on-one teacher-child interactions on one or more problems, (b) small-group instruction, and (c) whole-class instruction. Similarly, written-work artifacts come in multiple forms, such as (a) one child's work on a single problem, (b) multiple children's work on the same problem, and (c) one child's work on multiple problems, sometimes across time. The two types of artifacts can also be paired in that video episodes often have corresponding written work, and teachers can engage with both simultaneously or sequentially (e.g., explore the written work prior to watching the video).

Selection of video and written-work artifacts for showcasing children's thinking involves consideration of many factors. Sherin, Linsenmeier, and van Es (2009) provided guidance for selecting video, and many of these ideas can be applied to selecting written work as well. Specifically, they identified different types of clips that showcase children's thinking as well as three dimensions of video that will likely influence the discussion of the children's thinking depicted: (a) visibility of the children's mathematical thinking, (b) ease of understanding the children's ideas, and (c) extent to which the children are exploring substantive mathematical ideas.

Given the challenges of locating and selecting artifacts, fabricating written work that showcases particular ideas may be tempting, but we advise using authentic written work authored by children when possible. Children's work is endlessly fascinating and richly mathematical, and although we occasionally slightly adjust a piece of written work for particular purposes, we find restricting ourselves to authentic work beneficial. This approach keeps PD conversations grounded in what children actually do, and teachers appreciate this authenticity. Further, children show more variety in their strategies than we could ever generate ourselves, and this variety supports the customizable nature of our frameworks—teachers take ownership of these frameworks for themselves by interacting with authentic artifacts of children's thinking.

Evolution of Questioning Activities in RTEM PD

To help teachers increase their expertise in questioning to build on children's mathematical thinking, we brought children into the workshops for short, targeted activities like one-on-one interviews and small-group problem-solving sessions. Similar to the noticing activities, these questioning activities evolved over the course of the PD—both in terms of the complexity of the activities and the teachers' responsibilities within those activities.

Earlier Questioning Activities. When teachers first worked with the practice of questioning to build on children's thinking, we often designed activities that paired two teachers and one child in a problem-solving interview (as mentioned earlier). During the interview, teachers typically took turns posing problems to the child, and they supported each other in asking follow-up questions and determining what the child was saying and doing. After the interview, the teacher pairs debriefed their experiences by reflecting on the child's strategies and understanding as well as the questions they had posed during the interview.

In these earlier questioning activities, parts of the interview were simplified. For example, teachers did not need to generate their own problems to pose. Instead, they were given a list of problems from which to choose, and this list had limited variety in terms of problem types and number sets. Teachers were also given the broad purpose of exploring the child's thinking so that they had the freedom to follow the child's lead rather than feel as though they had to help the child reach a specific understanding. Further, to reinforce the idea that teachers should ground conversations in children's existing strategies, we started by providing a simplified version of our questioning framework that emphasized the questioning purpose of *exploring details of children's strategies.*

These earlier questioning activities were critical for piquing teachers' curiosity about children's thinking and helping them learn to ask questions that elicited children's ideas. For some teachers, the focus was new because these interviews were their first experiences interacting with a child with a focus on exploring the child's thinking rather than on leading him or her to correct answers or particular strategies.

Later Questioning Activities. Over the course of the multiyear PD, these questioning activities—like the noticing activities—evolved in two main ways. The first way was that the *complexity of the PD activity increased.* For example, in later questioning activities, we shifted from single interviews to double interviews. Pairs of teachers still worked together to interview a single child, but now they also interviewed the same child a second time, on two consecutive days. The goal for the double interview was to provide opportunities for teachers to practice questioning to both elicit and build on children's thinking. Specifically, when debriefing after the first interview, the teacher pairs planned how they would build on the child's thinking from the first interview during the second interview. First, they generated follow-up questions to ask the child about something he or she did during the first interview as a way to expand the *teachers'* understanding of the *child's* understanding. Second, they generated follow-up questions in which they posed new problems for the child to solve. These new problems were constructed on the basis of what the teachers had learned about the child's understanding in the first interview and as a way to test their ideas about that child's understanding or to extend it. After the second interview, the teacher pairs again debriefed their experiences, their evolving understanding of this child's understanding, and their questioning to elicit and build on the child's thinking.

Toward the end of the PD, we extended the complexity of our questioning activities even further—beyond conversations with one child—to provide opportunities for teachers to work on their questioning in small-group problem-solving sessions. Teachers again worked with children for 2 days, but the structure was different. On the first day, the PD activity began like many others—with a problem-solving interview to make sure that the instructional decisions were grounded in individual children's thinking. However, instead of interviewing a child with a partner, teachers generally interviewed by themselves in this questioning activity, but they had already engaged in multiple earlier activities involving partner interviewing. Next, about four teachers formed a group to debrief the thinking of the children they had interviewed. They used what they had learned about the children's thinking in the interviews to plan two problems to pose to the four children as a small group. One teacher then volunteered to serve as the teacher for a small-group problem-solving session with these four children while the other three teachers observed.

During the small-group problem-solving session, teachers supported and learned from one another. We adapted the idea of "teacher time-out" from Gibbons, Kazemi, Hintz, and Hartmann (2017), in that after the children had solved the problems the teachers had designed, the four teachers convened for a short conversation (5–10 minutes) away from the children, who were independently engaged in other activities (reading, drawing, etc.). During this "teacher time out" conversation, teachers reviewed the children's strategies for the two problems, chose one or more strategies as the focus for a sharing session with the small group, and generated possible questions to pose during that sharing session. The teachers then rejoined the children, and the volunteer teacher of the small group ran the sharing session while the other teachers observed. After the sharing session, the group of teachers again debriefed, reflecting on their evolving understanding of each child's understanding, their selection of strategies to showcase, and the questioning used to highlight the mathematics and keep children engaged. Note that in RTEM PD, our questioning activities with children in workshops did not extend beyond small-group problem-solving sessions, although we did address whole-class instruction elsewhere in the PD. However, some project-team members, in other settings, have extended the questioning activity so that teachers could collaborate in the context of whole-class instruction, thereby providing opportunities to explore questioning in both the circulating and sharing portions of lessons.

The second way that the questioning activities evolved was that the *teachers' responsibilities increased*. Teachers were not only encouraged to consider posing questions related to all five questioning purposes from the framework but also given more responsibility for generating and selecting problems to use. For example, for the interviews we asked teachers to select problems from longer and more varied lists that included multiple problem types and number sets, so that teachers had more choices and therefore had to exercise more judgment in tailoring their problems to individual children's understandings as they emerged in the interview. Eventually, we even asked teachers to generate some of the number sets themselves—we provided one number set for each potential problem and then asked teachers to generate easier and harder number sets before interviewing. Understanding the effects of categories of numbers (e.g., familiar fractions, unit fractions, etc.) with particular problem types and children's understandings is critical for responsive teaching. Teachers can select strategic number combinations so that children with various levels of understanding have access to problems and opportunities to advance their understandings in particular ways (Krause, Empson, & Jacobs, nd). However, this type of responsibility could have been overwhelming for teachers earlier in the PD.

Logistical Considerations for Questioning Activities. Additional planning is needed to schedule interactive experiences with children during workshops (e.g., interviews, small-group problem-solving sessions, etc.), but we have always found these activities to be worth the extra effort. First, children who can participate during a designated time frame will need to be identified. This task is made more complicated if the workshop meets during the summer (or on noninstructional days) or if the same child is needed to participate twice (when the activity moves beyond a single interview). Second, reserving multiple rooms for the teachers' work with children can be helpful because multiple conversations occurring simultaneously in a single room can be loud and confusing. Finally, we were able to schedule our double interviews and interview/small-group combinations on consecutive days. If having teachers out of the classroom for 2 consecutive days during the school year is problematic, these multiday activities could be adapted to occur in 1 day (morning and afternoon). In all logistical considerations, we encourage adaptation of the activities to fit contextual needs. The key is to be flexible, because the benefits of including children in workshops far outweigh any small concessions made to activity designs.

FINAL THOUGHTS

We join the other authors of this book in working to realize the potential in using frameworks of children's thinking (or learning trajectories) in PD. An understanding of the development of children's thinking over time is knowledge that is essential for teachers to be able to teach mathematics in ways that are responsive to children's thinking. However, as we have emphasized throughout the chapter, we believe that supporting teachers in learning only about children's thinking is insufficient. For teachers to learn to use this knowledge effectively in their classrooms, teachers must engage with frameworks of *both* children's thinking and instructional practices. They must also be encouraged to take ownership of and customize these frameworks based on the needs of their students and instructional contexts. We do not suggest that our specific frameworks are the only useful ones, but we do suggest that alone neither frameworks of children's thinking nor frameworks of instructional practices are sufficient for helping teachers gain expertise in responsive teaching, and, across our field, educators need more dialogue about other productive combinations.

The field also needs continued conversation about how to effectively support teachers in developing this expertise over time. Responsive teaching is challenging to enact, and teachers learn about the frameworks more quickly than they are able to integrate the frameworks into their instruction. Teachers therefore need numerous learning opportunities and support for multiple years—and simply extending the duration of PD is insufficient. The PD activities themselves need to evolve as teachers' expertise evolves over multiple years to allow teachers to experience more complexity and responsibility in the instructional practices the PD activities are designed to support. Using noticing and questioning activities, we provided two examples of this evolution from our RTEM PD, but we know that many other evolutions could be productive and further explorations of the possibilities are needed.

NOTE

This research was supported by the National Science Foundation (DRL-1712560), but the opinions expressed do not necessarily reflect the position, policy, or endorsement of the agency. We thank Teachers Development Group and their three facilitators who worked extensively with us. These facilitators were fantastic collaborators who worked tirelessly to help us conceptualize and implement the type of PD described in this chapter. We also thank the teachers who participated in our study for their commitment to improving mathematics teaching, as well as their generosity in constantly sharing their ideas and perspectives in their work with us.

REFERENCES

Ball, D. L., & Cohen, D. (1999). Developing practice, developing practitioners: Toward a practice-based theory of professional education. In L. Darling-Hammond & G. Sykes (Eds.), *Teaching as the learning profession: Handbook of policy and practice* (pp. 3–32). San Francisco, CA: Jossey-Bass.

Battey, D., & Chan, A. (2010). Building community and relationships that support critical conversations on race: The case of Cognitively Guided Instruction. In M. Q. Foote (Ed.), *Mathematics teaching and learning in K–12: Equity and professional development* (pp. 137–149). New York, NY: Palgrave MacMillan.

Cai, J. (2017). *Compendium for research in mathematics education.* Reston, VA: National Council of Teachers of Mathematics.

Carpenter, T. P., Fennema, E., Franke, M. L., Levi, L., & Empson, S. B. (2015). *Children's mathematics: Cognitively Guided Instruction* (2nd ed.). Portsmouth, NH: Heinemann.

Carpenter, T. P., Fennema, E., Peterson, P., Chiang, C., & Loef, M. (1989). Using knowledge of children's mathematics thinking in classroom teaching: An experimental study. *American Educational Research Journal, 26*(4), 499–531.

Carpenter, T. P., Franke, M. L., Johnson, N. C., Turrou, A. C., & Wager, A. A. (2016). *Young children's mathematics: Cognitively Guided Instruction in early childhood education.* Portsmouth, NH: Heinemann.

Carpenter, T. P., Franke, M. L., & Levi, L. (2003). *Thinking mathematically: Integrating algebra and arithmetic in elementary school.* Portsmouth, NH: Heinemann.

Design-Based Research Collective. (2003). An emerging paradigm for educational inquiry. *Educational Researcher, 32*(1), 5–8.

Empson, S. B. (2011). On the idea of learning trajectories: Promises and pitfalls. *The Mathematics Enthusiast, 8*(3), 571–596.

Empson, S. B., & Levi, L. (2011). *Extending children's mathematics: Fractions and decimals.* Portsmouth, NH: Heinemann.

Fennema, E., Carpenter, T., Franke, M. L., Levi, L., Jacobs, V. R., & Empson, S. B. (1996). Mathematics instruction and teachers' beliefs: A longitudinal study of using children's thinking. *Journal for Research in Mathematics Education, 27*(4), 403–434.

Franke, M. L., Carpenter, T. P., Levi, L., & Fennema, E. (2001). Capturing teachers' generative change: A follow-up study of professional development in mathematics. *American Educational Research Journal, 38*, 653–689.

Gay, G. (2002). Preparing for culturally responsive teaching. *Journal of Teacher Education, 53*(2), 106–116.

Gibbons, L. K., Kazemi, E., Hintz, A., & Hartmann, E. (2017). Teacher time out: Educators learning together in and through practice. *Journal of Mathematics Education Leadership, 18*(2), 28–46.

Grossman, P. (Ed.). (2018). *Teaching core practices in teacher education.* Cambridge, MA: Harvard Education Press.

Jacobs, V. R., & Ambrose, R. C. (2008). Making the most of story problems. *Teaching Children Mathematics, 15,* 260–266.

Jacobs, V. R., & Empson, S. B. (2016). Responding to children's mathematical thinking in the moment: An emerging framework of teaching moves. *ZDM–The International Journal on Mathematics Education, 48*(1–2), 185–197.

Jacobs, V. R., Franke, M. L., Carpenter, T. P., Levi, L., & Battey, D. (2007). Professional development focused on children's algebraic reasoning in elementary school. *Journal for Research in Mathematics Education, 38*(3), 258–288.

Jacobs, V. R., Lamb, L. L. C., & Philipp, R. A. (2010). Professional noticing of children's mathematical thinking. *Journal for Research in Mathematics Education, 41*(2), 169–202.

Jacobs, V. R., & Spangler, D. A. (2017). Research on core practices in K–12 mathematics teaching. In J. Cai (Ed.), *Compendium for research in mathematics education* (pp. 766–792). Reston, VA: National Council of Teachers of Mathematics.

Krause, G., Empson, S. B., & Jacobs, V. R. (nd). *Elementary school teachers' number choices for equal-sharing story problems.* (Unpublished manuscript.)

Ladson-Billings, G. (1995). Toward a theory of culturally relevant pedagogy. *American Educational Research Journal, 32*(3), 465–491.

McDonald, M., Kazemi, E., & Kavanagh, S. S. (2013). Core practices and pedagogies of teacher education: A call for a common language and collective activity. *Journal of Teacher Education, 64*(5), 378–386.

National Council of Teachers of Mathematics. (2014). *Principles to actions: Ensuring mathematical success for all.* Reston, VA: Author.

National Research Council. (2001). *Adding it up: Helping children learn mathematics.* Washington, DC: National Academy Press.

Pynes, D. (2018). *Teachers' collective noticing of children's mathematical thinking in self-facilitated collaborative inquiry* (Unpublished doctoral dissertation). University of Texas at Austin, Austin, TX.

Richards, J., & Robertson, A. D. (2016). A review of the research on responsive teaching in science and mathematics. In A. D. Robertson, R. E. Scherr, & D. Hammer (Eds.), *Responsive teaching in science and mathematics* (pp. 36–55). New York, NY: Routledge.

Sherin, M. G., Linsenmeier, K. A., & van Es, E. A. (2009). Selecting video clips to promote mathematics teachers' discussion of student thinking. *Journal of Teacher Education, 60*(3), 213–230.

Smith, M. S., & Stein, M. K. (2018). *5 practices for orchestrating productive mathematics discussions* (2nd ed.). Reston, VA: National Council of Teachers of Mathematics.

Turner, E. E., Foote, M. Q., Stoehr, K. J., McDuffie, A. R., Aguirre, J. M., Bartell, T., & Drake, C. (2016). Learning to leverage children's mathematical knowledge bases in mathematics instruction. *Journal of Urban Mathematics Education, 9*(1), 48–78.

CHAPTER 5

The Building Blocks and TRIAD Projects

Julie Sarama and Douglas H. Clements

Educational researchers have long complained that practitioners do not use the available evidence, and practitioners in turn bemoan the lack of research that provides practical solutions. Decades ago, we asserted that learning trajectories could close that gap in two critical educational activities that depend fundamentally on teachers, and therefore on professional development. The first was to build, and help teachers implement, a truly *research-based* curriculum. The second was to *scale up* implementation of the curriculum to entire districts. Each tells a story of using learning trajectories to support teachers. This chapter addresses these two critical activities by describing our development and research in two closely related projects focused on pre-K to 1st grade (with follow-up assessments many years thereafter). We describe each and then go into detail about what teachers learned and what we learned about using learning trajectories as the core of professional development efforts.

INTRODUCTION TO THE BUILDING BLOCKS AND TRIAD PROJECTS

Building Blocks was a National Science Foundation–funded project designed to provide resources so that all young children could build a solid foundation for mathematics (Clements & Sarama, 1998; Sarama & Clements, 2004). The proposal was to create research-based, technology-enhanced mathematics materials for pre-K through grade 2 with a focus on underserved children. We focused on building a complete curriculum for pre-kindergarten with software (another of our foci, Sarama & Clements, 2002) that extended from preschool to grade 2 and beyond.

When the research-and-development effort was ready to be scaled up, we created a research-based model: Technology-enhanced, Research-based, Instruction, Assessment, and Professional Development (TRIAD). We describe the processes of each of these efforts in the following sections.

The Curriculum Research Framework and Learning Trajectories

Our goal for Building Blocks was to create truly research-based curricula (Battista & Clements, 2000; Clements & Battista, 2000). However, both the ambiguities of the phrase "research-based instructional materials" and ubiquitous but weak claims that curricula are based on research (Clements, 2002, 2007; National Research Council, 2004; Senk & Thompson, 2003) led us to search for models that were genuinely scientific. Finding no clear, complete foundation for research-based curriculum development and evaluation, we created a Curriculum Research Framework (CRF) based on a synthesis of others and our previous work (see Clements, 2007). The CRF starts with reviews of research, invests substantial time and effort developing research-based learning trajectories, and then goes through multiple phases of formative assessment, working with small groups of children, then small groups of teachers, and finally scaling up to work with districts. The final summative evaluations also start small and expand (full details are available in Clements, 2002; Sarama & Clements, 2004).

There are two reasons learning trajectories play a foundational role in all of CRF's phases. First, learning trajectories are a device whose purpose is to support the development of a curriculum, or a curriculum component. The term *curriculum* stems from the Latin word for running, or course, referring to the course of experiences through which students grow to become mature adults. Thus, the notion of a path, or trajectory, has always been central to curriculum development and study. In his seminal work, Simon stated that a hypothetical learning trajectory included "the learning goal, the learning activities, and the thinking and learning in which the students might engage" (1995, p. 133).

Building on Simon's definition, but emphasizing a cognitive science perspective and a base of empirical research,

> We conceptualize learning trajectories as descriptions of children's thinking and learning in a specific mathematical domain, and a related, conjectured route through a set of instructional tasks designed to engender those mental processes or actions hypothesized to move children through a developmental progression of levels of thinking, created with the intent of supporting children's achievement of specific goals in that mathematical domain. (Clements & Sarama, 2004b, p. 83)

The second reason for learning trajectories' central role in the CRF is that they allow *teachers* to understand and build the mathematics of children (Steffe, 1991)—the thinking of children as it develops naturally. With an understanding of developmental progressions, teachers can be assured that all the goals and activities outlined are within the developmental capacities of their students. They can understand and use the knowledge that each level provides a natural developmental building block to the next level—a sine qua non for effective use of the strategy of formative assessment. Finally, they can be committed and guided to providing the mathematical building blocks for school success, because the research on which they are based typically involves children who have had educational advantages that allow them to do well at school.

The Learning Trajectories

Because the original objective was to create complete curricula, we needed to create LTs addressing all of the important mathematical topics for our intended audience, children from preschool to grade 2. To determine these topics, we considered what particular mathematics is culturally valued (Clements, Sarama, & DiBiase, 2004; National Governor's Association Center for Best Practices & Council of Chief State School Officers, 2010; National Council of Teachers of Mathematics, 2006) as well as research on what constituted the core ideas and skill domains of mathematics for young children, with an emphasis on topics that were mathematical foundational, generative for, and interesting to young children (Clements, Sarama, & DiBiase, 2004). One of the reasons underlying the name we gave to our project was our desire that the materials emphasize the development of basic mathematical building blocks—ways of knowing the world mathematically—organized into two domains: (a) numeric and quantitative and (b) spatial and geometric. Research shows that young children are endowed with intuitive and informal capabilities in both these domains (Sarama & Clements, 2009). Three mathematical themes were woven through both these main domains: patterning, classifying data, and sorting and sequencing. That is, although we included specific activities for each theme (e.g., sequential patterns such as ABCABCABC), we emphasized these areas as mathematical *processes* that applied across topics (National Research Council, 2009). For example, there is a "plus one" pattern in counting. This pattern links counting and addition. There are spatial patterns in shape composition, and so forth.

With topics and LT goals established, we then engaged in the most arduous task, creating the developmental progressions for each LT. We began with extensive reviews of the research, interpreting and synthesizing disparate types of research conducted with different children at different ages (Clements & Sarama, 2007a; Sarama & Clements, 2009). These tentative progressions then had to be formatively evaluated and refined. This is an intensely iterative and dynamic process, employing, depending on the quality and quantity of the existing research, techniques such as grounded theory methods, clinical interviews, and teaching experiments (Clements, 2007).

Further, because we were designing curricula, we needed to organize each topic into *complete* LTs—and we believe this is critical for building effective professional development. As described previously, complete learning trajec- tories have three interrelated components, a goal, a developmental progres- sion of levels of thinking, and instructional activities correlated to each level (Clements & Sarama, 2004a, 2014a; Sarama & Clements, 2009). Thus, to at- tain a certain mathematical competence in a given topic or domain (the goal), students learn each successive level (the developmental progression), aided by tasks (instructional activities) designed to build the mental actions-on-objects that enable thinking at each higher level. (As in the original formulation, Si- mon [1995], we include instruction as an integral component, compared to some uses of the term LT that only address the developmental progression.) We believe the power and uniqueness of the learning trajectories construct, especially for professional development and teaching, stem from the inex- tricable interconnection between all three components. Therefore, starting with the developmental progressions, we again reviewed an often different and wider literature—from academic research to that capturing the wisdom of expert practice—on effective instructional tasks and strategies to promote *each* level of *each* developmental progress. Once again, these had to be for- matively evaluated and refined using a variety of approaches, mainly teaching experiments and design experiments (Clements, 2007). This created the first draft of curricular components for preschool (ages 3 and 4 years) to grade 2.

History and Goals

We proposed to develop Building Blocks at a time when the field was recogniz- ing both the importance of mathematics to young children and the dearth of instructional materials available for early mathematics (see reviews in Balfanz, 1999; Clements & Sarama, 2007a). Subsequent research supported this no- tion. For example, because mathematics predicts later mathematics as well as later reading (Duncan et al., 2007; Duncan & Magnuson, 2011), mathematics appears to be a core component of cognition (Clements & Sarama, 2011).

Because early childhood teachers often have limited preparation and neg- ative attitudes toward this important topic (Copley, 2004; Sarama & DiBiase, 2004), effective professional development in early mathematics is critical. This is especially so given the diverse settings, diverse workforces in early childhood (Institute of Medicine [IOM] and National Research Council [NRC], 2015) and even antipathy toward mathematics in the earliest years, with some educators resisting or rejecting any "academic" intervention (Cle- ments & Sarama, 2014b).

As stated, the goal of the Building Blocks project was to create *a tru- ly evidence-validated* curriculum. It would be reasonable to assume such a curriculum is easily available because developers and publishers frequent- ly characterize their curricula as *based* on research. However, the ubiqui- ty and multifariousness of such characterizations, in conjunction with the ambiguous nature of the phrase "research-based," makes such claims suspect. The CRF and its core of learning trajectories supported all aspects of the curriculum, from building activity sequences to support for users—that is, built-in professional development.

DESIGN OF THE PROFESSIONAL DEVELOPMENT FOR TRIAD

The final phase of the CRF involves scaling up the intervention. Doing this successfully involved far more guidance than what was included in the CRF. Based on syntheses of theories and research in the fields of implementation and scale-up, we created the Technology-enhanced, Research-based, Instruction, Assessment, and professional Development (TRIAD) model. The most important part of this model involved professional development, and we designed comprehensive professional development based on learning trajectories for TRIAD. We describe the TRIAD model and the research relevant to professional development in the following section.

Although specific interventions in early mathematics have been successful (Clements & Sarama, 2011), few have been brought to scale successfully, especially across the challenging diversity of populations and contexts in the early childhood system in the United States. We developed a theoretically based scale-up model for early mathematics (Sarama, Clements, Starkey, Klein, & Wakeley, 2008) that has avoided the pollution and dilution that often plagues efforts to achieve broad success (Sarama & Clements, 2017).

The main goals of the TRIAD PD were for teachers to learn to use learning trajectories to engage young children in appropriate but challenging mathematical experiences . . . and then do it! That is, the ultimate goal was for teachers to implement the learning trajectories in the Building Blocks curriculum with fidelity to increase their students' engagement and learning of mathematics.

Background: A Brief History of TRIAD

The overarching theoretical framework for our research and development of a scale-up model is an elaboration of the Network of Influences framework (Sarama, Clements, & Henry, 1998). For the purposes of this chapter, we note the centrality of the teacher and the supports for the teacher. For example, professional development strongly influences teacher knowledge, which then impacts implementation fidelity, which in turn affects children. Support from coaches also has a strong effect on teachers' knowledge and practice, while other factors, such as support from school leaders and physical resources, are influential, but to a more moderate degree.

Two sources propelled and shaped these ideas into the TRIAD model. First was the growing body of research on successfully scaling up interventions

(Sarama et al., 2008). Second was the results of a National Science Foundation (NSF) planning grant to Sarama, "Planning for Professional Development in Pre-School Mathematics." Teachers' voices were the main influences on that plan (see Sarama, 2002). There we learned what teachers wanted and believed was effective, as well as such details as preferred locations and scheduling for PD. Synthesizing these, we created 10 guidelines that define the TRIAD model.

TRIAD Guidelines. These 10 guidelines form a coherent whole, so we summarize them all briefly, elaborating and documenting only those most relevant for this book: the learning trajectory and professional development guidelines (#4 and #5—for a full explication and research review for all 10, see Sarama & Clements, 2013; Sarama et al., 2008). We believe that they are a "coherent whole" in two complementary but inverse ways. First, learning trajectories pervade the model—they are the core of TRIAD and therefore are relevant to every guideline. Second, all the guidelines should be considered in planning any professional development project, as its ultimate success—improved mathematics education for students—depends on coordination among multiple stakeholders and supports for teachers.

1. *Involve and promote communication among key groups around a shared vision of the innovation.* This institutionalizes the intervention, for example in the case of ongoing socialization and professional development of new teachers.

2. *Promote equity* through equitable allocation of resources and use of curriculum and instructional strategies that have demonstrated success with underrepresented populations.

3. *Plan for the long term.* Recognizing that scale-up is not just an increase in number, but also of complexity, provide continuous, adaptive support over an extended period of time. Plan an incremental implementation and use dynamic, multilevel feedback and self-correction strategies.

4. *Focus on instructional change that promotes depth of children's thinking, placing learning trajectories at the core* of the teacher/child/curriculum triad to ensure that curriculum, materials, instructional strategies, and assessments are aligned with (a) national and state standards and a vision of high-quality education, (b) each other, and (c) "best practice" as determined by research, including formative assessment (Ball & Cohen, 1999; Bodilly, 1998; Bryk, Sebring, Allensworth, Suppescu, & Easton, 2010; Fullan, 2000; Kaser, Bourexis, Loucks-Horsley, & Raizen, 1999; National Mathematics Advisory Panel, 2008; Raudenbush, 2008; Sowder, 2007). This guideline is important for implementation with fidelity at any scale, although alignment is increasingly important at larger scales.

5. *Provide professional development that is ongoing, intentional, reflective, goal-oriented, focused on content knowledge and children's thinking, grounded in particular curriculum materials, and situated in the classroom and the school.* A focus on content includes accurate and adequate subject-matter knowledge both for teachers and for children. A focus on children's thinking emphasizes the learning trajectories' developmental progressions and their pedagogical application in formative assessment. Grounding in particular curriculum materials should include all three aspects of learning trajectories, especially their connections. This also provides a common language for teachers in working with each other and with other groups (Bryk et al., 2010). "Situated in the classroom" does not imply that all training occurs within classrooms. However, off-site intensive training remains focused on and connected to classroom practice and is completed by classroom-based enactment with coaching. In addition, this professional development should encourage sharing, risk taking, and learning from and with peers. Aim at preparing to teach a specific curriculum and develop teachers' knowledge and beliefs that the curriculum is appropriate, and its goals are valued and attainable. Situate work in the classroom, formatively evaluating teachers' fidelity of implementation and providing feedback and support from coaches in real time (e.g., Bryk et al., 2010; Elmore, 1996; Guskey, 2000; Hall & Hord, 2001; Pellegrino, 2007; Showers, Joyce, & Bennett, 1987). As with #4, this guideline is important for implementation with fidelity at any scale. However, the planning, structures, common language, formative evaluation, and school-level context are increasingly important as the implementation moves to larger scales.

6. *Build expectations and camaraderie to support a consensus around adaptation. Establish and maintain cohort groups.* Facilitate teachers visiting successful implementation sites. Build local leadership by involving principals and encouraging teachers to become teacher leaders.

7. *Ensure school leaders are a central force supporting the innovation and provide teachers continuous feedback that children are learning what they are taught and that these learnings are valued.* Leaders, especially principals, must show that the innovation is a high priority, through statements, resources, and continued commitment to permanence of the effort.

8. *Give latitude for adaptation to teachers and schools but maintain integrity.* Emphasize the similarities of the curriculum with sound practice and what teachers already are doing. Help teachers distinguish productive adaptations from lethal mutations (Brown & Campione, 1996).

9. *Provide incentives for all participants, including intrinsic and extrinsic motivators linked to project work,* such as external expectations—from standards to

validation from administrators. Show how the innovation is advantageous to and compatible with teachers' experiences and needs.

10. *Maintain frequent, repeated communication, assessment ("checking up"), and follow-through efforts at all levels within each school district, emphasizing the purpose, expectations, and visions of the project, and involve key groups in continual improvement through cycles of data collection and problem solving.*

Design Principles. The TRIAD guidelines provide the overarching principles for the design of the professional development. Success with our Building Blocks and TRIAD (scale-up) projects is arguably largely attributable to the focus on learning trajectories (Clements & Sarama, 2008), as TRIAD guidelines #4 and #5 state. Several other projects also report success with variations of that approach (Bright, Bowman, & Vacc, 1997; Wright, Martland, Stafford, & Stanger, 2002). Also consistent with the "ongoing" aspect of #5 is the intensity and extent of the PD. All of these projects included far more extensive and intensive professional development than the usual 1-day workshop, with the PD for these projects ranging from 5 to 14 full days. TRIAD's guideline #5 includes that PD should be "grounded in particular curriculum materials." Of course, if you want teachers to use learning trajectories, the curriculum must be based on learning trajectories (such as in *Building Blocks*).

Task Design and Sequencing

Because our learning trajectories were created in the context of curriculum development and scale-up projects, they were always intended to be used by teachers. That is, such embeddedness intrinsically designs the learning trajectories with connection to practice. However, there are several issues on LTs we had to address before they were ready for use in large-scale professional development.

Considerations of Grain Size. Although we respect projects that have used large grain sizes with success, such as the growth points of our Australian colleagues (e.g., B. A. Clarke, 2004; D. M. Clarke et al., 2001), in our view, developmental progressions are best designed with a more detailed grain size to support curriculum development and teaching. That is, our vision was to have each level represent a qualitatively distinct pattern of thinking but one that is a reasonable goal for the next curricular step—that is, within the Zone of Proximal Development (Vygotsky, 1935/1978) of children at their present level.

We believe our results with this grain size have been successful, especially because each time a new activity or substantial modification of an activity occurs within the curriculum, it signals a goal of a new level of thinking. For example, we found that teachers could easily master the developmental progression for subitizing, given the reasonable number of levels and the nature of the advance from perceptual to conceptual (seeing parts and synthesizing them into a whole) subitizing. However, other topics were more complex. For those, we have made an innovation recently that was motivated by the concern that teachers were a bit lost and may have forgotten the "big picture." Therefore, we maintained the fine grain size for teaching, but help teachers see the "forest and trees" of each *major* LT, where "trees" were each level of the learning trajectory's developmental progression, and the "forest" is the broad category, providing the "big picture" of the major phases. Figure 5.1 presents an example for the LT for shapes.

Another recent decision, prompted by our extension of the LTs to infants and toddlers, was to be consistent with our view of learning trajectories as always building on children's strengths. Our earliest levels were often names "Pre-Composer" or the like. This may have given the impression that a child had no competencies on which to build. In Figure 5.1, the first level, which used to be called "Pre-Recognizer," was changed to "'Same Thing' Comparer: Foundations."

We also corrected what we now consider a mistake in our fine grain sizes. Our original learning trajectories included all developmental levels, including those that were not instructional targets. For example, in comparing the number of objects in sets, research has identified a level in which children count each set, but if the set with fewer has physically larger objects, will still maintain that set has "more." Despite its developmental veracity, we found some teachers thought they should *teach* children that level. Thus, we eliminated all such "non-instructional" levels. We did not ignore the research, but simply combined the description of that behavior into the prior contiguous level, rather than making it a separate level. This allowed teachers to know such behaviors may occur but helped them avoid thinking of these sets of behaviors as an instructional objective.

Number of LTs. Because our first goal was to develop an LT-based curriculum, we developed LTs for every major topic for early mathematics. Given we would embed those LTs within all components of the curriculum (print, software, and so forth), this would provide the greatest research guidance with minimum strain on teachers. That is, we hoped that they would read about an LT in the curriculum, but in the worst case (without such reading or without PD), they could implement the activities as they were realized in the curriculum and enact the LT, possibly learning from those actions and from children's responses.

However, as we planned the PD for the teachers, this issue emerged again. Here we made the decision to spend most PD hours on a handful of *major* topics, such as counting, subitizing, comparing, arithmetic,

Figure 5.1. Samples from an Early Childhood Learning Trajectory for 2D Geometric Shapes

Broad Category	Developmental Progression Levels	Examples of Instructional Activities
Foundations	"Same Thing" Comparer: Foundations *Says two pictures of houses are the same or different.*	Talk about similarities and differences of any objects, focusing on their shapes.
	Shape Matcher	*Match Shapes.* With a small group, use familiar (prototypical) shapes in two colors; give each child a shape from one color. Choose a shape from the other color that otherwise exactly matches a child's shape. Ask children who has an exact match for your shape. Follow up by asking how the child knows his or her shape is a match.
Visual Thinker	Shape Recognizer—Typical *"It's a rectangle because it looks like a door."*	*Circle Time!* Have children sit in the best circle they can make. Show and name a large, flat circle, such as a hula hoop. As you trace the circle with your finger, discuss how it is perfectly round; it is a curved line that always curves the same. Ask children to talk about circles they know, such as those found in toys, buildings, books, tricycles, or bicycles, and clothing.
	Shape Matcher—More Shapes	*Match Shapes.* As above, but using a wider variety of shapes from the shape set in different orientations.
	Shape Recognizer—Circles, Squares, and Triangles +	*Is It or Not?* Draw a triangle on a surface where the entire class can view it. Ask children to name it, and then tell why it is not a circle. Draw a non-triangle (e.g., having a fourth very short side). Ask children what it looks like, and then ask them to tell why it is not a triangle. Repeat.

Figure 5.1. Samples from an Early Childhood Learning Trajectory for 2D Geometric Shapes (continued)

Broad Category	*Developmental Progression Levels*	*Examples of Instructional Activities*
Parts	Side Recognizer *Correctly identifies and counts parts of shapes.*	*Mystery Pictures.* Computer activity in which children identify a shape given a description.
	Constructor from Parts—Exact	*Build Shapes.* Children use straws of different lengths to construct different shapes with exact representation.
Property	Shape Property Identifier *"It's a rectangle because the four sides are parallel and there are 4 right angles."*	*Guess My Rule.* Children guess the sorting rule by watching the teacher sort a pile of shapes.

Source: Clements, D. H., & Sarama, J. (2016/2019). Learning and teaching with learning trajectories— [LT]2. Retrieved from Marsico Institute, Morgridge College of Education, University of Denver website: http://LearningTrajectories.org

and geometric shapes. Shorter sessions were given to other topics when the weeks focusing on those topics were reached, including length measurement and patterning. Less PD time was given to other topics, although we did include simple short instructions and then curriculum-provoked reminders regarding sorting and classifying, spatial orientation (other spatial skills were embedded throughout), multiplication, disembedding geometric figures, area, volume, and angle. (This approach is consistent with the AMTE Standards for Mathematics Teacher Preparation [Association of Mathematics Teacher Educators, 2017] that recommended that [in the report, preservice] teachers learn one or two learning trajectories deeply at first and then have resources to learn others.)

Connections Among LTs. We originally designed each LT to be embedded in a matrix, in which each column was an LT and levels were aligned developmentally across LTs. We did not abandon that format, but we were forced away from it—by publishers. Neither the publishers of the Building Blocks curriculum nor of our books like the matrices, and they separated them. In retrospect, we did gain a focus on "one LT at a time" that helped teachers avoid feeling (even more) overwhelmed at the amount of new information. However, we lost the interconnectedness in the original print materials. Instead, we slowly introduced such connections in subsequent professional development sessions.

TRIAD Professional Development

As stated, our learning trajectories were created in the context of curriculum development and developing a scale-up model, so they were designed to be understandable and useable by teachers. We followed TRIAD guidelines in designing extensive and intensive professional development. Each session addresses learning trajectories for each mathematics topic; using the developmental progression for observation and other authentic formative assessment strategies; supporting mathematical development in the classroom; recognizing and supporting mathematics throughout the day; setting up mathematics learning centers; teaching with computers (including use of the management system and research-based teaching strategies); small-group activities; and supporting mathematical development in the home. The sessions include hands-on experience in rooms set up to mirror the structure of early childhood classrooms, with an emphasis on interactions with peers around common issues. We provide a concrete example toward the end of this section.

Supporting Teachers' Learning of Learning Trajectories. Here, we emphasize teachers' learning of the three components of learning trajectories. For the *goal,* we engaged teachers in discussions and activities that developed their understanding of the mathematics content including—but also going well beyond—the content in the curriculum. Thus, teachers learned the fundamental content of number, arithmetic, geometry, measurement, and early algebraic reasoning (e.g., see Chapter 2 of National Research Council, 2009). This content included "profound understanding" (Ma, 1999) of the mathematics they were to teach and a good deal beyond. As a brief example of a challenging topic, they learned not only proper names for geometric shapes (beyond what they initially considered the "basic four"—circle, square, triangle, rectangle) and defining properties of those shapes, but also about hierarchies of shape classification and propagation of properties in those schemes. The latter is not content that they would teach but does prevent such pedagogical and logical errors as refusing to accept a square when children are asked to "find rectangles in the room."

Similarly, teachers engaged in presentations, discussions, and experiences to learn about the other two components of LTs, the developmental progressions and the instructional activities. The main technological tool providing these experiences was the *Building Blocks Learning Trajectory (BBLT)* web application. *BBLT* provided scalable access to the learning trajectories via descriptions, videos, and commentaries. Each aspect of the learning trajectories—*developmental progressions* of children's thinking and connected *instruction*—is linked to the others. The BBLT application was designed to encourage teachers to view the LTs through a curriculum or developmental perspective and then connect them. That is, teachers might choose an activity and not only see an explanation and video of the activity "in action," but also immediately see the level of thinking that activity is designed to develop, in the context of the entire LT.

A second generation of that tool, the Learning and Teaching with Learning Trajectories [LTLT, aka (LT)^2 or simply LT2, see http://LearningTrajectories.org] provides learning trajectories based mathematics resources for professional development experts, coaches, teachers, caregivers, and parents, including for the first time, those *not* served by any present means, who are ill-equipped to provide high-quality mathematical experiences, especially in the communities of vulnerable children. LT2 runs on all technological platforms, addresses new ages—birth to age 8 years—and includes new alignments with standards and assessments, as well as new software for children.

Another unique aspect of LT2 is the built-in technology "games" that not only help children learn and help adults understand the mathematics goals and children's achievements of them, but automatically collect information on children's level of thinking, allowing all future interactions to be individualized. (We are seeking funding to supplement LT2 with "push texts" to generate interest and guide and maintain use. Texts would be informed by localization research on target populations, so they are customized and relevant to those communities, such as games that allow interactions to be personalized and individualized.)

Work with tools such as LT2 that connect all three parts of an LT helps teachers build in multiple, linked representations of, and perspectives on, complex phenomena that research shows is necessary for successfully applying concrete cases and the theories in which they are embedded in ill-structured domains (Feltovich, Spiro, & Coulson, 1997). The resulting cognitive flexibility positively impacts the variety of teaching strategies that people develop and ease with which they acquire new repertoires (Showers et al., 1987).

LT2 thus provides professional development by bringing participating teachers into a practical, close discourse around "best practice" classrooms, including instruction and assessment. LT2 is used in four related ways. First, it aids presentations of the trajectories and activities to teachers. Second, teachers observe, react to, and discuss specific trajectory levels, activities, or the relationship between a trajectory level and an activity. Third, coaches and mentors use the site in talking to teachers, often in their classrooms, about the trajectories, activities, or the relationship between the two. This is especially valuable in situations in which a teacher says, or demonstrates, that she or he did not fully understand a given activity's goals or structure. Fourth, teachers may voluntarily consult LT2 when they wish to refresh their memories on a particular activity they are to teach or to delve more deeply into understanding their children's thinking.

Discussions of LT2's best practice videos make explicit how such practice exemplifies research-based principles and will emphasize that even exemplary teachers continue to struggle—illustrating that high-quality teaching for understanding is both rewarding and challenging, and that everyone can continue to improve and contribute to the profession (Heck, Weiss, Boyd, & Howard, 2002; Weiss, 2002). Such virtual visits and discussion communicate the vision of the curriculum in action and make the ideas and processes accessible, memorable, engaging, and therefore usable.

Brief Example of a Session. Consider a day focused mainly on geometry. The day might start with an interactive session with all teachers. They engage in a warm-up exploration of two-dimensional shapes through an activity in which one teacher in a pair secretly hides a shape from a set and, without using its name, describes it so well that their partner can choose the congruent shape from an identical set. An interactive presentation follows, developing teachers' knowledge of these shapes. For example, asked to define a rectangle, a ubiquitous response is "two long sides and two short sides." An intense discussion follows, as they discover that many shapes (e.g., that of a kite) fit that description but are not rectangles, and others do not fit the description (e.g., squares) but are rectangles. These struggles are related to children's learning of geometry, and videos and discussions are used to paint the landscape of the developmental progression for children's learning of 2D shapes (recall Figure 5.1). Finally, the teachers play the role of children in the "whole group" activities (e.g., *Circle Time!* or *Is It or Not?* in Figure 5.1) and then discuss them. Questions include: What level of thinking for this LT is this intended to teach? Why and how was it designed to teach that level?

For the next few hours, teachers engage in hands-on experience in rotating among other areas of the professional development space set up to mirror the structure of early childhood classrooms: small group, learning centers, and a computer center. At each, they take turns implementing the activities in the learning trajectories based curriculum, interacting with peers around common issues. For example, they take turns leading a "whole group" (1/4 of the teachers) in one of the activities and then discuss it (e.g., *Circle Time!* or *Is It or Not?* in Figure 5.1). Similarly, in the "small group," teachers work in teams of four, taking turns leading a small-group activity (e.g., *Match Shapes* or *Build Shapes* in Figure 5.1). Here the other participants play the role of children operating at different levels of the LT and the teacher fills out a Small Group Record Sheet on each of them. They discuss these and then rotate the roles. In learning centers, teachers explore materials laid out and discuss how they would use them to develop the targeted levels of thinking. In the computer centers, they work with the instructional activities on computers. They also work individually or in pairs on LT2, following a guide that directs their work and attention to issues and questions emerging from specific videos, and also exploring the LT2 resource on their own.

At the conclusion, teachers describe what they have learned about the learning trajectories and children. They also share ideas on how to enhance or adapt the activities they learned (productive adaptations, not lethal mutations!).

Coaching. Coaches and mentors work with teachers throughout the 2-year period, visiting teachers in their classrooms at least once per month. Coaching reminds teachers that the project is a priority, that a commitment has been made to it, and that somebody cares about them (Hord, Rutherford, Huling-Austin, & Hall, 1987). The TRIAD coaching model is dynamic and is based on research (Bay-Williams & McGatha, 2014; Germeroth & Sarama, 2017; Luebeck & Burroughs, 2017), and we believe extends the complex research corpus (Luebeck & Burroughs, 2017) by showing that learning trajectories can serve as an effective core of coaching too. Initial questionnaire data are helpful, but not sufficient, for knowing who will need additional assistance from coaches and mentors. For example, some teachers present themselves well and even misrepresent how much of the curriculum they are teaching; only coaching visits reveal and address such problems. With apologies to Leo Tolstoy, all happy classes resemble one another, but each unhappy class is unhappy in its own way (Teddlie & Stringfield, 1993). Therefore, we created a dynamic model in which additional attention by both mentors and coaches is given immediately until adequate fidelity of implementation is achieved. Several additional features also encourage sensitivity to individual needs of teachers, including (a) time to learn and work with cohort groups; (b) job-embeddedness—addressing concrete, immediate concern with practical problems of implementation; (c) opportunities for practice, receiving *individual,* nonthreatening feedback from coaches; and (d) software and LT2 resources that facilitate individualization. Mentors will also coach teachers and will complete implementation fidelity evaluations and give immediate feedback to teachers on those evaluations.

In summary, the TRIAD/*Building Blocks* professional development follows research-based guidelines and provides a combination of experiences. As we shall see, multiple studies indicate it has had strong positive effects on both teachers and their children.

Evaluation: Pilot for Scale-up Research

Our first study was an early research and development effort—not a scale-up, but a proof of concept (Sarama et al., 2008). Within a design involving only 25 classrooms serving children at risk for later school failure, we examined the impact of the model, using newly created measures of fidelity of implementation, classroom observations of mathematics environment and teaching, and child outcomes. High levels of fidelity of implementation resulted in consistently higher scores in the intervention, compared to control classes on the observation instrument, and significantly and substantially greater gains in children's mathematics achievement in the intervention, compared to the control children (effect size = 0.62 standard deviations, which raises a 50th percentile child to the 73rd percentile). We refined the TRIAD PD based on these experiences.

Evaluation: Methods of Full Scale-up Study

Schools and Participants. For the true scale-up evaluation, 42 schools serving low-resource communities in two cities, Buffalo, NY, and Boston, MA, were randomly selected and randomly assigned to three treatment groups using a randomized block design involving 1,375 preschoolers in 106 classrooms. The two treatment groups differed only in that one included a follow-through component that was to be implemented when the children moved to kindergarten and 1st grade; therefore, at the pre-K level, the focus of this chapter, there were only two distinct groups, with two-thirds of the schools in TRIAD group and one-third in the control group.

Based on the pilot, we decided to engage preschool teachers in 2 full days of professional development during the summer, 3 days during the school day in the fall and 3 days during the spring for the first year and 5 full days for the second year of the project. We used the full TRIAD Professional Development plan described in the previous section.

Assessing Fidelity: Beyond Compliance. We designed a fidelity tool when first evaluating the Building Blocks curriculum. Even in this nascent form, we included, but also moved beyond, *compliance* fidelity. That is, insisting that teachers follow a strict calendar for the weeks of the curriculum would not be consistent with the learning trajectories approach. Further, the form increases scores for productive adaptations (e.g., surface changes to fit a class's theme) but does decrease scores for lethal mutations (in which the learning trajectory is changed in a matter deleterious to learning, such as making an appropriately challenging activity too simple [Brown & Campione, 1996]). We refined this instrument when designing the TRIAD scale-up model, notably adapting it to uses beyond assessments for research purposes to those that focused exclusively on professional development.

Thus, we actually designed two observational instruments to address "deep change" that "goes beyond surface structures or procedures to assess teachers' beliefs, norms of social interaction, and pedagogical principles as enacted in the curriculum" (Coburn, 2003, p. 4). One was the Fidelity instrument—appropriate only for the teachers using Building Blocks, and the other was a more general measure for any curriculum, permitting experimental-control comparisons, the "Classroom Observation of Early Mathematics—Environment and Teaching" (COEMET). Both were created based on research on the characteristics and teaching strategies of effective teachers of early childhood mathematics (e.g., D. M. Clarke & Clarke, 2004; Clements & Conference Working Group, 2004; Fraivillig, Murphy, & Fuson, 1999; Galván Carlan, 2000). An example of a Likert item (with response possibilities from strongly disagree to strongly agree) shared by the instruments in the "Mathematical Focus" section is:

> The teacher began by engaging and focusing children's mathematical thinking (i.e., directed children's attention to, or invited them to consider, a mathematical question, problem, or idea).

Also shared by both instruments in the section for an interactive mathematics activity entitled "Organization, Teaching Approaches, Interactions" are items with the subheadings "expectations," "eliciting children's solution methods," "supporting children's conceptual understanding," and so forth.

The Fidelity instrument evaluates the degree to which teachers taught the intervention curricula; thus it addresses adherence and integrity to a specific program but is sufficiently general to apply to either of the two specific intervention curricula. An example of an item unique to the Fidelity measure in the "Organization, Teaching Approaches, Interactions" section is:

> The teacher conducted the activity as written in the curriculum or made positive adaptations to it (not changes that violated the spirit of the core mathematical activity).

An example of one of the COEMET'S three items in a section unique to this measure, "Personal Attributes of the Teacher," is:

> The teacher appeared to be knowledgeable and confident about mathematics (i.e., demonstrated accurate knowledge of mathematical ideas and procedures, demonstrated knowledge of connections between, or sequences of, mathematical ideas).

Evaluation: Results of Full Scale-up Study

Evidence of Teachers' Effectiveness: Children's Learning Along the LTs. The
TRIAD classes significantly outperformed the comparison group, with an effect size of 0.72 (Clements & Sarama, 2007b). The topics on which TRIAD children made the largest gains relative to the control children, such as shape, shape composition, counting, and comparing number, were those in which research supported the construction of accurate, elaborated learning trajectories at the level of the children's mathematical development. TRIAD children made less of a gain compared to control children on topics for which the LT was based on less research, such as comparing shapes, or for which we did not posit a developmental progression, such as naming numerals.

Fidelity: The TRIAD Teachers. Results indicate that teachers implemented the intervention with good fidelity—quite literally, as on the 5-point Likert scale items, with −2 as Strongly Disagree and +2 as Strongly Agree, the mode was 1 in both fall and spring, and the mean was 0.77 in fall and 0.86 in spring (Clements & Sarama, 2007b). Less than 15% of teachers had an average below 0.50 (about 6% were negative). This result is similar to that observed in previous research with the same instrument and curriculum. For example, the mean in one study was 3.0, equal to Agree in a smaller-scale study using a Likert scale from 1 to 4 (Clements & Sarama, 2008). Note that the slight difference between the two results is due to the addition of "0" as a neutral option, leading to smaller positive means. This provides evidence that interventions in preschool mathematics education, such as this one, can be successfully implemented on a large scale if a research-based model is used.

COEMET: Comparing TRIAD and Control Teacher. TRIAD classes had higher scores than the control classes on overall Classroom Culture, Specific Mathematics Activities (SMA), the total number of mathematics activities observed, and the number of computers on and working for students to use. However, the group differences and influences of these differed.

The Classroom Culture score was the best predictor of child achievement. This score assesses teachers' general approach to mathematics education, indicated by "environment and interaction" variables such as responsiveness to children, use and mathematization of "teachable moments," as well as "personal attributes of the teacher" variables, including appearing knowledgeable and confident about mathematics as well as showing enjoyment in, curiosity about, and enthusiasm for, teaching mathematics. These variables suggest that the learning trajectories based PD successfully altered teachers' beliefs and dispositions, beyond specific curriculum practices. Such practices were also positively affected, given that teachers used the computer component of the Building Blocks curriculum and engaged their children in a greater number of explicit, targeted, mathematics activities.

TRIAD teachers also had higher scores for the SMA subscale, suggesting that their instruction was of higher quality than those in the control classrooms. However, the difference between the TRIAD and control groups was small, and the score was not a statistically significant mediator. This was disappointing, because we hypothesized that the TRIAD PD would help teachers enact LT-based strategies, such as formative assessment. It may be that such strategies take considerable time to internalize or that the PD needs to more extensively emphasize these strategies.

The substantial difference in the number of mathematics activities observed in SMAs raised the issue of whether this variable was a proxy for total time allocated to mathematics activities. To differentiate and compare these variables, we calculated the total number of minutes during which children were experiencing mathematics during the visit. The mean time on task was

27 minutes for control, and 32 minutes for TRIAD, which was not significantly different. This suggests that children learn more from a variety of activities emphasizing the same level of thinking, beyond simply more "time on task." That is, they may learn concepts more readily from generalizing mathematics structures from different problematic situations that require the same mathematical concepts and processes (e.g., mental actions-on-objects) for their solution. Further, such multiple situations may create a greater number of cognitive paths for retrieval of these concepts and processes.

There was no evidence that TRIAD was differentially effective for girls and boys, or children with or without IEPs. There was evidence that the intervention was differentially effective for only a single ethnic/racial comparison: African American children learned less than other children in the same control classrooms, and African American children learned more than other children in the same Building Blocks classrooms. It may be that TRIAD is particularly effective in ameliorating the negative effects of low expectations for African American children's learning of mathematics.

Sustainability

Even when researchers study long-term effects of an early intervention, the focus is usually on the persistence of child outcomes. We have investigated this issue (not relevant here, but see Clements et al., 2018), but our colleagues are often surprised when we claim that the long-term effect of greater importance is *sustainability*—the continued use of program components in the achievement of desirable student outcomes and professional practice over time, with a focus on the maintenance of core beliefs and values, and the use of these core beliefs to guide adaptability (Clements et al., 2015). Successful scale-up requires not only consequential implementation but also endurance over long periods of time. Without sustainability, the challenging implementation efforts affect only a small slice of the student population. With sustainability, the effects are a continuous wave of benefits for many more children and for eventual institutionalization of the intervention.

We evaluated the fidelity of implementation and the sustainability of TRIAD (Clements et al., 2015). Of the initial 72 participants, 14 had retired or were assigned to a different grade level. Although a logical expectation would be that, after the cessation of external support and professional development provided by the intervention, teachers would show a pattern of decreasing levels of fidelity, these teachers actually demonstrated *increasing* levels of fidelity, continuing to demonstrate high levels of sustained fidelity in their implementation of the underlying curriculum 2 years past exposure. Different profiles of variables predicted separate aspects of sustainability, but one variable was by far the strongest and most consistent predictor: child gain in mathematics achievement. Teachers who (accurately) perceived greater gain in mathematics within their classroom demonstrated higher levels of fidelity across the study's time frame.

Perceptions of their children's learning may motivate teachers to continue to implement all components of the intervention and to productively face challenges such as those they may face with technology.

In a second wave of evaluation, *6 years* after the end of the intervention, teachers continued to demonstrate sustained or increasing levels of fidelity (Sarama, Clements, Wolfe, & Spitler, 2016). Notable is these teachers' encouragement and support for discussions of mathematics and their use of formative assessment. Also, on a survey almost all TRIAD teachers (control teachers were not studied) agreed with each statement about learning trajectories:

I believe my own greater understanding of the learning trajectories has
. . .

* improved student outcomes in math. (100%)
* given me new instructional activities that I still use. (98%)
* increased my comfort level teaching early childhood math. (98%)
* resulted in my own greater individualization in mathematics instruction. (98%)

A caveat is that many teachers left pre-K by the time of this survey and so data was available for only 28 teachers, and it may have been that the most enthusiastic ones remained.

In summary, the learning trajectory based instruction engaged in by the prekindergarten teachers in this study may have provided a coherent program of teaching and learning, which promoted the significant levels of fidelity found in this study. Teachers taught the curriculum with increasing fidelity as time went by, even though research project staff were no longer able to provide support. They seemed to have internalized the program. By engaging in the initial professional development, and then becoming empowered by their own knowledge of the trajectories and the practices to support learners through the trajectories, they became progressively more faithful to the intended program, instead of drifting from it as time elapsed and support disappeared, a contrasting negative trend found in other studies.

DESIGNERS LEARNING THROUGH PD IMPLEMENTATION: PRINCIPLES, PITFALLS, PROMISES, AND POTENTIAL

Across our studies of TRIAD, certain factors appear particularly important for an effective scale-up effort (Sarama & Clements, 2013). Our evaluations indicate that effectiveness depends on the development of teachers' skills and knowledge (i.e., *TRIAD guideline #5*). A total of 50 to 70 hours of professional development—we provide about 75 hours—is consistent with previous research documenting what is necessary to achieve measurable effectiveness (Yoon, Duncan, Lee, Scarloss, & Shapley, 2007). Situating the materials not just in the classroom but also in each school is important for related but additional reasons. Because it establishes a cultural practice and provides peer support, school-based implementation supports both fidelity and sustainability of a new curriculum (Zaslow, Tout, Halle, Vick, & Lavelle, 2010) and reaches more than 90% of students in the school (not just one classroom, hoping for "spillover").

Learning trajectories played a critical role in both teachers' and children's learning (guideline #4). From the creation of the TRIAD model to the present instantiations, we have continually lessened lectures and increased interactions. For example, we now present and discuss videos for 10–15 minutes, then engage in small-group activities, share out, and repeat the cycle.

Finally, respect for teachers by project staff and the resultant acceptance of in-class support from coaches and technology support staff appeared to be as or more important than whole-group professional development sessions. Note that this was especially striking in another project, just being completed, in which we used coaches employed by the school district. They were not able to schedule meetings regularly, and our initial impression is that they were not as effective. If valid, this has serious ramifications for scaling up coaching-intensive models.

An additional lesson learned was that we created additional formats for the classroom observation tools. For example, we created an "iFidelity" form for use by coaches and teachers. It simply changed the grammatical structure to say, for example, "I began by engaging and focusing children's mathematical thinking." More important, everyone understood that no one but the teacher and coach would see the completed forms. This form contributed to the efficacy of the coaching visits and increased self-directed professional development.

Other supportive aspects of the TRIAD model were also important. First is the use of scientifically validated early childhood interventions. Some early childhood educators romanticize the individual teacher's interpretation and even creation of the educational program. Our work and that of many others suggests that implementation of systematic, scientifically based practice is more effective than private, idiosyncratic practice (Raudenbush, 2009). This does not imply use of a "scripted" curriculum, and any such approach contradicts TRIAD's use of learning trajectories in the service of formative assessment and its insistence on adaptation to local conditions (guideline #8). Rather, focusing on the shared scientific base is a more effective and efficient way to improve education. Further, such scientifically grounded shared practice is, somewhat paradoxically, more likely to generate creative contributions. Teachers may modify shared practices and those modifications will be accessible to discussion and further research.

Second was the consistent communication with and among all key groups. Project activities would not be achieved without consistent communication and continued collaboration (see guidelines #1, #7, and #10).

We found it necessary to repeatedly provide higher-level administrators with updates and reminders of the projects' goals and activities. Similarly, every change in administration had to be monitored and new people introduced to the project and its successes quickly. The early introduction of the project was facilitated by prior awareness of the researchers' work and a strong commitment to achieving the project goals. It is a challenge to institutionalize such continuous commitments within each district. Presentations of the evaluations and corresponding discussions of how to maintain the implementation infrastructure within the organization appeared to have positive effects on sustainability. Also significant was the implementation team's consistent efforts to involve supervisors and coordinators in professional development sessions, classroom visits, and separate meetings. Such involvement created essential advocates for the intervention within the organizations.

In summary, a coherent model of professional development, curriculum, instruction, and assessment based on learning trajectories may provide the conditions for promoting sustainability in teacher practices and may be particularly beneficial in addressing the climate of low expectations in urban schools, as teachers increase their understanding of the capacities of all children to learn mathematics.

WHAT PITFALLS DO PRESENT AND FUTURE EFFORTS FACE? WHAT LESSONS WERE LEARNED?

Having districts maintain the model for new teachers has been a serious challenge. Even districts that collaborated on generating the research that showed the effectiveness of the model and the necessity of it asked us to provide a 2-hour workshop to replace the 12 days of professional development! Thus, we must as a field communicate more effectively on the necessity of following a *scale-up model with fidelity,* including its professional development components, as well as implementing any curriculum or any other intervention with fidelity.

Our observational data show that teachers find it difficult to use learning trajectories to implement effective formative assessment. We have increased PD activities where this is practiced (e.g., asking teachers to bring in their small-group record sheets, and work together to plan the next set of activities on that topic) as well as similar coaching, but as yet do not know if these changes will be effective.

We are tracking diffusion within, but especially to, surrounding districts. The availability of teacher trainers and independent coaches was especially crucial at one site, as they were asked by administrators of nearby school districts who had heard about the implementation to build new implementation teams within their districts. Having in-house leaders (e.g., early childhood and mathematics supervisors or coordinators) organize and lead such teams is not only logistically important but also promotes positive spread and shift in ownership. Not attending to such features may lead to a poor implementation and thus contribute to the too-frequent phenomenon of a salient success followed by "copies" that are less successful—erroneously changing the perception of the effectiveness of the intervention.

NOTE

This research was supported by the Institute of Education Sciences, U.S. Department of Education, through grants R305K05157 and R305A110188 and also by the National Science Foundation, through grants ESI-9730804 and REC-0228440. The opinions expressed are those of the authors and do not represent views of the IES or NSF. Although the research is concerned with the scale-up model, not particular curricula, a minor component of the intervention used in this research has been published by the authors, who thus could have a vested interest in the results. An external auditor oversaw the research design, data collection, and analysis, and other researchers independently confirmed findings and procedures. The authors wish to express appreciation to the school districts, teachers, and students who participated in this research.

REFERENCES

Association of Mathematics Teacher Educators. (2017). *AMTE standards for mathematics teacher preparation*. Raleigh, NC: Author.

Balfanz, R. (1999). Why do we teach young children so little mathematics? Some historical considerations. In J. V. Copley (Ed.), *Mathematics in the early years* (pp. 3–10). Reston, VA: National Council of Teachers of Mathematics.

Ball, D. L., & Cohen, D. K. (1999). *Instruction, capacity, and improvement*. Philadelphia, PA: Consortium for Policy Research in Education, University of Pennsylvania.

Battista, M. T., & Clements, D. H. (2000). Mathematics curriculum development as a scientific endeavor. In A. E. Kelly & R. A. Lesh (Eds.), *Handbook of research design in mathematics and science education* (pp. 737–760). Mahwah, NJ: Erlbaum.

Bay-Williams, J. M., & McGatha, M. B. (2014). *Mathematics coaching: Resources and tools for coaches and leaders, K–12*. Boston, MA: Pearson Education.

Bodilly, S. J. (1998). *Lessons from New American Schools' scale-up phase: Prospects for bringing designs to multiple schools*. Santa Monica, CA: RAND Education.

Bright, G. W., Bowman, A. H., & Vacc, N. N. (1997). Teachers' frameworks for understanding children's mathematical thinking. In E. Pehkonen (Ed.), *Proceedings of the 21st Conference of the International Group for the Psychology of Mathematics Education* (Vol. 2, pp. 105–112). Lahti, Finland: University of Helsinki.

Brown, A. L., & Campione, J. C. (1996). Psychological theory and the design of innovative learning environments: On procedures, principles, and systems. In R. Glaser (Ed.), *Innovations in learning: New environments for education* (pp. 289–325). Mahwah, NJ: Erlbaum.

Bryk, A. S., Sebring, P. B., Allensworth, E., Suppescu, S., & Easton, J. Q. (2010). *Organizing schools for improvement: Lessons from Chicago.* Chicago, IL: University of Chicago Press.

Clarke, B. A. (2004). A shape is not defined by its shape: Developing young children's geometric understanding. *Journal of Australian Research in Early Childhood Education, 11*(2), 110–127.

Clarke, D. M., Cheeseman, J., Clarke, B., Gervasoni, A., Gronn, D., Horne, M., . . . Sullivan, P. (2001). Understanding, assessing and developing young children's mathematical thinking: Research as a powerful tool for professional growth. In J. Bobis, B. Perry, & M. Mitchelmore (Eds.), *Numeracy and beyond (Proceedings of the 24th Annual Conference of the Mathematics Education Research Group of Australasia, Vol. 1)* (pp. 9–26). Reston, Australia: MERGA.

Clarke, D. M., & Clarke, B. A. (2004). Mathematics teaching in grades K–2: Painting a picture of challenging, supportive, and effective classrooms. In R. N. Rubenstein & G. W. Bright (Eds.), *Perspectives on the teaching of mathematics (66th yearbook)* (pp. 67–81). Reston, VA: National Council of Teachers of Mathematics.

Clements, D. H. (2002). Linking research and curriculum development. In L. D. English (Ed.), *Handbook of international research in mathematics education* (pp. 599–636). Mahwah, NJ: Erlbaum.

Clements, D. H. (2007). Curriculum research: Toward a framework for "research-based curricula." *Journal for Research in Mathematics Education, 38*(1), 35–70. doi:10.2307/30034927

Clements, D. H., & Battista, M. T. (2000). Designing effective software. In A. E. Kelly & R. A. Lesh (Eds.), *Handbook of research design in mathematics and science education* (pp. 761–776). Mahwah, NJ: Erlbaum.

Clements, D. H., & Conference Working Group. (2004). Part one: Major themes and recommendations. In D. H. Clements, J. Sarama, & A.-M. DiBiase (Eds.), *Engaging young children in mathematics: Standards for early childhood mathematics education* (pp. 1–72). Mahwah, NJ: Erlbaum.

Clements, D. H., & Sarama, J. (1998). *Building Blocks—Foundations for mathematical thinking, pre-kindergarten to grade 2: Research-based materials development.* Buffalo, NY: State University of New York at Buffalo.

Clements, D. H., & Sarama, J. (Eds.). (2004a). Hypothetical learning trajectories [Special issue]. *Mathematical Thinking and Learning, 6*(2).

Clements, D. H., & Sarama, J. (2004b). Learning trajectories in mathematics education. *Mathematical Thinking and Learning, 6,* 81–89. doi:10.1207/s15327833mtl0602_1

Clements, D. H., & Sarama, J. (2007a). Early childhood mathematics learning. In F. K. Lester, Jr. (Ed.), *Second handbook of research on mathematics teaching and learning* (Vol. 1, pp. 461–555). New York, NY: Information Age Publishing.

Clements, D. H., & Sarama, J. (2007b). Effects of a preschool mathematics curriculum: Summative research on the *Building Blocks* project. *Journal for Research in Mathematics Education, 38*(2), 136–163.

Clements, D. H., & Sarama, J. (2007/2013). *Building Blocks, Volumes 1 and 2.* Columbus, OH: McGraw-Hill Education.

Clements, D. H., & Sarama, J. (2008). Experimental evaluation of the effects of a research-based preschool mathematics curriculum. *American Educational Research Journal, 45*(2), 443–494. doi:10.3102/0002831207312908

Clements, D. H., & Sarama, J. (2011). Early childhood mathematics intervention. *Science, 333*(6045), 968–970. doi:10.1126/science.1204537

Clements, D. H., & Sarama, J. (2014a). *Learning and teaching early math: The learning trajectories approach* (2nd ed.). New York, NY: Routledge.

Clements, D. H., & Sarama, J. (2014b, March 3, 2014). Play, mathematics, and false dichotomies. Preschool matters . . . today! Retrieved from preschoolmatters. org/2014/03/03/play-mathematics-and-false-dichotomies/

Clements, D. H., Sarama, J., & DiBiase, A.-M. (2004). *Engaging young children in mathematics: Standards for early childhood mathematics education.* Mahwah, NJ: Erlbaum.

Clements, D. H., Sarama, J., Layzer, C., Unlu, F., Wolfe, C. B., Fesler, L., . . . Spitler, M. E. (2018). *Effects of TRIAD on mathematics achievement: Long-term impacts.* Manuscript submitted for publication.

Clements, D. H., Sarama, J., Wolfe, C. B., & Spitler, M. E. (2015). Sustainability of a scale-up intervention in early mathematics: Longitudinal evaluation of implementation fidelity. *Early Education and Development, 26*(3), 427–449. doi:10.1080/1040928 9.2015.968242

Coburn, C. E. (2003). Rethinking scale: Moving beyond numbers to deep and lasting change. *Educational Researcher, 32*(6), 3–12.

Copley, J. V. (2004). The early childhood collaborative: A professional development model to communicate and implement the standards. In D. H. Clements, J. Sarama, & A.-M. DiBiase (Eds.), *Engaging young children in mathematics: Standards for early childhood mathematics education* (pp. 401–414). Mahwah, NJ: Erlbaum.

Duncan, G. J., Dowsett, C. J., Claessens, A., Magnuson, K., Huston, A. C., Klebanov, P., . . . Japel, C. (2007). School readiness and later achievement. *Developmental Psychology, 43*(6), 1428–1446. doi:10.1037/0012-1649.43.6.1428

Duncan, G. J., & Magnuson, K. (2011). The nature and impact of early achievement skills, attention skills, and behavior problems. In G. J. Duncan & R. Murnane (Eds.), *Whither opportunity? Rising inequality and the uncertain life chances of low-income children* (pp. 47–70). New York, NY: Russell Sage.

Elmore, R. F. (1996). Getting to scale with good educational practices. *Harvard Educational Review, 66,* 1–25.

Feltovich, P. J., Spiro, R. J., & Coulson, R. L. (1997). Issues of expert flexibility in contexts characterized by complexity and change. In P. J. Feltovich, K. M. Ford, & R. R. Hoffman (Eds.), *Expertise in context: Human and machine* (pp. 125–146). Cambridge, MA: The MIT Press.

Fraivillig, J. L., Murphy, L. A., & Fuson, K. C. (1999). Advancing children's mathematical thinking in Everyday Mathematics classrooms. *Journal for Research in Mathematics Education, 30*(2), 148–170.

Fullan, M. G. (2000). The return of large-scale reform. *Journal of Educational Change, 1,* 5–28.

Galván Carlan, V. (2000). *Development of an instrument to assess the use of developmentally appropriate practices in teaching mathematics in early childhood classrooms.* (Doctoral dissertation). University of Houston, Houston, TX.

Germeroth, C., & Sarama, J. (2017). Coaching in early mathematics. *Advances in Child Development and Behavior, 53,* 127–168. doi:10.1016/bs.acdb.2017.03.002

Guskey, T. R. (Ed.). (2000). *Evaluating professional development.* Thousand Oaks, CA: Corwin Press.

Hall, G. E., & Hord, S. M. (2001). *Implementing change: Patterns, principles, and potholes.* Boston, MA: Allyn & Bacon.

Heck, D. J., Weiss, I. R., Boyd, S., & Howard, M. (2002, April). *Lessons learned about planning and implementing statewide systemic initiatives in mathematics and science education.* Paper presented at the American Educational Research Association, New Orleans, LA. www.horizon-research.com/public.htm

Hord, S. M., Rutherford, W., Huling-Austin, L., & Hall, G. E. (1987). *Taking charge of change.* Alexandria, VA: Association for Supervision and Curriculum Development.

Institute of Medicine (IOM) and National Research Council (NRC). (2015). *Transforming the workforce for children birth through age 8: A unifying foundation.* Washington, DC: National Academy Press.

Kaser, J. S., Bourexis, P. S., Loucks-Horsley, S., & Raizen, S. A. (1999). *Enhancing program quality in science and mathematics.* Thousand Oaks, CA: Corwin Press.

Luebeck, J., & Burroughs, E. (2017). A research journey through mathematics coaching. *The Journal of Mathematical Behavior, 46,* 152–162. doi:10.1016/j.jmathb.2016.11.004

Ma, L. (1999). *Knowing and teaching elementary mathematics: Teachers' understanding of fundamental mathematics in China and the United States.* Mahwah, NJ: Erlbaum.

National Council of Teachers of Mathematics. (2006). *Curriculum focal points for prekindergarten through grade 8 mathematics: A quest for coherence.* Reston, VA: Author.

National Governor's Association Center for Best Practices & Council of Chief State School Officers. (2010). *Common core state standards initiative K–12 standards development teams.* Retrieved from https://www.nga.org/files/live/sites/NGA/files/pdf/2010COMMONCOREK12TEAM.PDF

National Mathematics Advisory Panel. (2008). *Foundations for success: The final report of the National Mathematics Advisory Panel.* Washington DC: U.S. Department of Education, Office of Planning, Evaluation and Policy Development.

National Research Council. (2004). *On evaluating curricular effectiveness: Judging the quality of K–12 mathematics evaluations.* Washington, D.C.: Mathematical Sciences Education Board, Center for Education, Division of Behavioral and Social Sciences and Education, The National Academies Press.

National Research Council. (2009). *Mathematics learning in early childhood: Paths toward excellence and equity.* Washington, DC: National Academy Press. doi:10.17226/12519

Pellegrino, J. W. (2007). From early reading to high school mathematics: Matching case studies of four educational innovations against principles for effective scale up. In B.

Schneider & S.-K. McDonald (Eds.), *Scale up in practice* (pp. 131–139). Lanham, MD: Rowman and Littlefield.

Raudenbush, S. W. (2008). Advancing educational policy by advancing research on instruction. *American Educational Research Journal, 45*, 206–230.

Raudenbush, S. W. (2009). The *Brown* legacy and the O'Connor challenge: Transforming schools in the images of children's potential. *Educational Researcher, 38*(3), 169–180. doi:10.3102/0013189X09334840

Sarama, J. (2002). Listening to teachers: Planning for professional development. *Teaching Children Mathematics, 9*(1), 36–39.

Sarama, J., & Clements, D. H. (2002). *Building Blocks* for young children's mathematical development. *Journal of Educational Computing Research, 27*(1&2), 93–110. doi:10.2190/F85E-QQXB-UAX4-BMBJ

Sarama, J., & Clements, D. H. (2004). *Building Blocks* for early childhood mathematics. *Early Childhood Research Quarterly, 19*, 181–189.

Sarama, J., & Clements, D. H. (2009). *Early childhood mathematics education research: Learning trajectories for young children.* New York, NY: Routledge.

Sarama, J., & Clements, D. H. (2013). Lessons learned in the implementation of the TRIAD scale-up model: Teaching early mathematics with trajectories and technologies. In T. G. Halle, A. J. Metz, & I. Martinez-Beck (Eds.), *Applying implementation science in early childhood programs and systems* (pp. 173–191). Baltimore, MD: Brookes.

Sarama, J., & Clements, D. H. (2017). Interventions in early mathematics: Avoiding pollution and dilution. *Advances in Child Development and Behavior, 53*, 95–126. doi:10.1016/bs.acdb.2017.03.003

Sarama, J., Clements, D. H., & Henry, J. J. (1998). Network of influences in an implementation of a mathematics curriculum innovation. *International Journal of Computers for Mathematical Learning, 3*, 113–148.

Sarama, J., Clements, D. H., Starkey, P., Klein, A., & Wakeley, A. (2008). Scaling up the implementation of a pre-kindergarten mathematics curriculum: Teaching for understanding with trajectories and technologies. *Journal of Research on Educational Effectiveness, 1*(1), 89–119. doi:10.1080/19345740801941332

Sarama, J., Clements, D. H., Wolfe, C. B., & Spitler, M. E. (2016). Professional development in early mathematics: Effects of an intervention based on learning trajectories on teachers' practices. *Nordic Studies in Mathematics Education, 21*(4), 29–55.

Sarama, J., & DiBiase, A.-M. (2004). The professional development challenge in preschool mathematics. In D. H. Clements, J. Sarama & A.-M. DiBiase (Eds.), *Engaging young children in mathematics: Standards for early childhood mathematics education* (pp. 415–446). Mahwah, NJ: Erlbaum.

Senk, S. L., & Thompson, D. R. (2003). *Standards-based school mathematics curricula. What are they? What do students learn?* Mahwah, NJ: Erlbaum.

Showers, B., Joyce, B., & Bennett, B. (1987). Synthesis of research on staff development: A framework for future study and a state-of-the-art analysis. *Educational Leadership, 45*(3), 77–87.

Simon, M. A. (1995). Reconstructing mathematics pedagogy from a constructivist perspective. *Journal for Research in Mathematics Education, 26*(2), 114–145. doi:10.2307/749205

Sowder, J. T. (2007). The mathematical education and development of teachers. In F. K. Lester, Jr. (Ed.), *Second handbook of research on mathematics teaching and learning* (Vol. 1, pp. 157–223). New York, NY: Information Age Publishing.

Steffe, L. P. (1991). Mathematics curriculum design: A constructivist's perspective. In L. P. Steffe & T. Wood (Eds.), *International perspectives on transforming early childhood mathematics education* (pp. 389–398). Hillsdale, NY: Erlbaum.

Teddlie, C., & Stringfield, S. (1993). *Schools make a difference: Lessons learned from a 10-year study of school effects.* New York, NY: Teachers College Press.

Vygotsky, L. S. (1978). *Mind in society: The development of higher psychological processes.* Cambridge, MA: Harvard University Press. (Original work published 1935).

Weiss, I. R. (2002, April). *Systemic reform in mathematics education: What have we learned?* Paper presented at the Research presession of the 80th annual meeting of the National Council of Teachers of Mathematics, Las Vegas, NV.

Wright, R. J., Martland, J., Stafford, A. K., & Stanger, G. (2002). *Teaching number: Advancing children's skills and strategies.* London, United Kingdom: Paul Chapman/ Russell Sage.

Yoon, K. S., Duncan, T., Lee, S. W.-Y., Scarloss, B., & Shapley, K. L. (2007). *Reviewing the evidence on how teacher professional development affects student achievement* (Issues & Answers Report, REL 2007–No. 033). Retrieved from ies.ed.gov/ncee/edlabs/ regions/southwest/pdf/REL_2007033.pdf

Zaslow, M. J., Tout, K., Halle, T. G., Vick, J., & Lavelle, B. (2010). *Toward the identification of features of effective professional development for early childhood educators: A review of the literature.* Retrieved from www2.ed.gov/rschstat/eval/professional-development/ literature-review.pdf

Design Considerations for Professional Development Involving Learning Trajectories

P. Holt Wilson and Paola Sztajn

This book focuses on professional development (PD) that promotes learning trajectory based instruction, a model of teaching where instructional decisions are informed by research on student learning. Like Ms. Williams from Chapter 1, teachers engaged in this form of instruction use frameworks of student thinking in a variety of teaching practices, from setting goals and selecting tasks to leading discussions and assessing learning. Teachers in PD involving LTs and frameworks for student thinking can learn to use LTs to create, select, and adapt instructional tasks and anticipate how students might engage with them. LTs can assist teachers in noticing the details of students' thinking, posing questions to extend their thinking, preparing for and leading mathematics discussions, and adjusting instruction in response to student learning. Overall, teachers in PD involving LTs learn about LTs and seek ways to improve instruction through using these frameworks to attend to students during their teaching.

The chapters in this book make a compelling case that LTs can be useful tools for teaching that is centered on student thinking and, in addition to outlining what teachers learned, they detail each project's process for designing PD. Because reports of research on PD often fail to provide detailed descriptions of the actual design of the program under analysis (Sztajn, 2011), the chapters in this book are unique in their explicit and extended attention to design. They provide an opportunity to identify similarities and differences across several PD programs that can further our understanding of how to develop effective PD involving LTs and thus support PD designers as they prepare to work with teachers around LTs.

An important similarity across all projects, and one that should be at the forefront for PD designers, is each PD program's respect for teachers and their knowledge. For example, the Learning Trajectory Based Instruction (LTBI; Chapter 2) PD program is guided by a commitment to positioning teachers as knowers. The program considers PD an opportunity to bring together researchers and teachers in conversations about student thinking and LTs. Researchers in the Children's Measurement project (Chapter 3) conceive of their work as an ongoing dialogue with prospective, practicing, and retired teachers. They see themselves as teacher researchers who engage teachers in the research process within their own classrooms. The Responsive Teaching in Elementary Mathematics (RTEM; Chapter 4) project emphasizes teachers' professionalism by encouraging teachers to take ownership of and customize the frameworks introduced in the PD. Researchers purposefully design PD activities that evolve in complexity as teachers' expertise evolves over time.

Finally, in the Building Blocks and Technology-enhanced, Research-based, Instruction, Assessment, and Professional Development projects (TRIAD, Chapter 5), teachers are regarded as key in the implementation of an innovative, research-based curriculum. It is part of the researchers' guidelines that PD be designed to encourage teacher sharing, risk-taking, and learning from their peers. Attending to the researcher–teacher relation and respecting teachers' knowledge are, therefore, at the core of each of these PD programs. All projects were designed with explicit attention to engaging teachers in experiences that build on their existing knowledge and promote their learning of student thinking.

Another important similarity across all projects is the way each PD is situated in the practice of teaching. The importance of grounding PD in practice is well known among PD designers, and all programs described in this book make use of artifacts from practice such as student work, videos, assessments, and mathematical tasks. The programs also include opportunities for teachers to experiment with the PD ideas in their own classrooms and contexts. Designed to closely connect with teaching, each PD program includes opportunities for teachers to use student thinking as a part of their daily work with students and learn from their own practice.

Respecting teachers as knowers and situating PD in practice are important general features of quality PD design. For the remainder of this chapter, we examine three additional PD design features identified and discussed in the preceding chapters that we see as important for and specific to quality PD that involves LTs. First, when introducing LTs to teachers, it is important to present the LTs in ways that are amenable to teaching. Thus, PD designers should consider the representations used to support teacher learning. Second, PD involving LTs should attend to the ways in which LTs can be used in the practice of teaching. As PD designers and facilitators work with teachers around LTs, the connections between these frameworks and the actual day-to-day work of teaching cannot be taken for granted; rather, these connections need to be explicitly discussed in the PD. And third, although PD involving LTs can build upon teachers' prior knowledge and contexts to promote more equitable instruction, the use of LTs does not necessarily translate into the kind of ambitious instruction envisioned in Chapter 1. Attention to understanding teachers and their working environments is needed when connecting LTs to equitable instruction.

REPRESENTING LTs FOR TEACHERS

When designing and revising their PD, each project in this book worked to represent LTs in ways that were accessible, meaningful, and helpful for teachers. LTs are an abstract idea that can take different forms, serve different purposes, and highlight particular aspects of a concept while obscuring others. Thus, each chapter addresses the ways in which the project attended to how to best represent LTs for teachers. Particularly for LTs designed by researchers with goals other than teaching, the need to attend to what representations are appropriate for use in PD contexts is not surprising and speaks to the importance of representations when designing PD around LTs.

Representations of LTs initially used by some projects foregrounded features of LTs that teachers did not find relevant or useful for teaching. For example, the Children's Measurement project discusses how the formal language and details of student thinking of LTs published for research audiences were barriers for teachers and impeded their learning. In response, the project collaborated with teachers across multiple implementations of their PD to refine descriptions of the LT levels to make them more recognizable for teachers. The TRIAD project eliminated some "non-instructional" levels and incorporated the behaviors into prior levels to signal to teachers that, although such behaviors might occur, they are not instructional objectives. These projects show the importance of attending to teachers as they work with LT representations and making adjustments when needed.

The changes in these LTs might have emerged from a feature of the representations used in both of these projects: The Children's Measurement and the TRIAD projects use LTs with very detailed descriptions of students' behaviors, given their focus on what Sarama and Clements characterize as curricular steps. Their LTs' representations, therefore, tend to use small grain–size levels that can support the parsing of instructional activities. The RTEM project uses frameworks that have a small number of larger grain–size categories, which they consider central for teachers' in-the-moment use of these frameworks in the classroom. The LTBI project, on the other hand, combines smaller and larger grain sizes through the creation of markers that group smaller grain–size levels of an LT into larger chunks.

Despite differences in the grain size of the LTs and frameworks presented to teachers, what these projects show is the importance of considering teachers as the end users of representations of LTs presented in PD. Developing or adapting LTs to support teacher learning requires attention not only to what teachers can make sense of and use in the PD setting, but also to how useful and easy these representations are for supporting instruction in the classroom. Thus, each of the projects in this book attended to what teachers are doing in practice when designing and, when needed, refining the representations of LTs or frameworks used in PD. We contend that the attention to the user and to the uses of the LTs in teaching, together with PD designers' willingness to revise initial representations when they seemed problematic in practice, supported teacher learning in these projects.

Another issue to be considered concerning LT representations and PD design is the number of mathematical concepts addressed and the number of LTs or frameworks used in the various programs. Whereas LT representations typically focus on one mathematical concept, students use several concepts when learning a new one. Given the interconnectedness of mathematical ideas, how can PD around LTs address these connections? In their unique ways, all PD programs discussed the use of more than one framework of student thinking in their programs. Using and connecting different representations was one way these programs dealt with the need to support teachers as they learn about LTs and continue to attend to student mathematical learning broadly. Thus, the PD programs presented in this book also attend to the ways in which representations support teachers' overall understanding of their students as learners.

For example, the LTBI PD program discusses LTs for place value, counting, addition and subtraction, ordering, and comparing numbers in its later iterations. To address these several LTs, the designers use a table created to represent connections across the content topics that portray broader profiles of students as mathematical learners. The Children's Measurement project focuses on LTs on length, area, and volume to address their content goal of geometric measurement. With their focus on curriculum, the TRIAD project focuses most of its PD on major LTs such as counting, subitizing, comparing, arithmetic, geometric shapes, measurement, patterning, and others. After addressing each of these major LTs to make the content accessible for teachers, PD designers introduce connections among the LTs in later PD sessions. The RTEM project focuses on fractions and uses two frameworks of student thinking in their PD: a problem-type and a strategy framework. Although these two frameworks are different in their mathematical scope than other LTs, it is the interaction across these different representations that supports teachers' understanding of student learning. These examples suggest that multiple LTs or frameworks of student thinking can be needed to capture students as mathematical learners in ways that allow teachers to support their students.

As the projects in this book show, sharing LTs with teachers is not a trivial task, and straightforward presentations of some published accounts of LTs may not support teachers in finding ways to use LTs to accomplish their goals for teaching and understandings students. When designing PD involving LTs, it is important to consider what the LTs highlight in their representations, assess the ways each representation is useful for different aspects of teaching, and establish connections among representations. Further, it is important to continue to attend to whether the representations used in the PD are, in fact, supporting teachers' communication about students' mathematics learning, understanding of students as mathematical learners, and implementation of instruction that is centered on student thinking. Without proper representations, LTs run the risk of not supporting teacher learning. Therefore, PD designers are tasked with carefully attending to the representations of LTs they choose and the ways in which these representations can actually serve as a useful tool for teachers.

CONNECTING LTs AND TEACHING

As a map of student thinking over time, LTs are useful for diagnosing a student's current understanding and identifying the next learning goal that is likely to be productive. However, many provide little guidance on how to actually orchestrate instruction in ways that support students in refining their current understanding toward the next learning goal. Consequently, all PD programs described in this book provide opportunities for teachers to explicitly connect LTs and teaching. The chapters offer two different approaches to linking LTs with teaching in PD settings: working with mathematical tasks and introducing frameworks for instruction. These approaches go beyond the goal of situating the PD in the practice of teaching as examined earlier in this chapter: They speak directly to the need to explicitly consider different components of what constitutes ambitious instruction described in Chapter 1 when designing PD involving LTs.

A focus on mathematical tasks engages teachers in using LTs to analyze problems and consider what makes them more or less appropriate for particular students in specific teaching situations. The need for this attention to tasks seems to be important even in PDs that work with LTs that, by definition, include tasks. Each of the programs included a focus on mathematical tasks as a key feature of their PD. For example, some PD activities from the LTBI and Children's Measurement projects utilize teachers' existing curriculum materials and focus on using LTs to select and adapt tasks or lessons from these materials as a way to connect LTs with teaching. In these cases, the LTs serve as a framework for task analysis to help determine their potential for addressing specific learning goals supported by the LTs. In the RTEM project, PD activities focus on using their frameworks of student thinking to create or select problems appropriate for a student's current understanding. The TRIAD PD focuses on using the *Building Blocks* curriculum to learn about the LTs underlying the curriculum. The curriculum is developed to specifically connect LTs and teaching, and teachers examine tasks presented in the materials to link them with associated levels of the LT.

The other approach to connecting LTs and teaching involves introducing frameworks of instructional practice in conjunction with the LTs. In Chapter 4, RTEM researchers assert that frameworks of student thinking alone are insufficient for teachers to develop responsive teaching practices, and the researchers describe their use of two frameworks of instructional practice to assist teachers in noticing children's thinking and questioning to build on children's thinking. This need for frameworks of instruction is also discussed in the other chapters. The LTBI project uses the *5 Practices for Orchestrating Productive Mathematics Discussions* (Smith & Stein, 2011) as a way to create opportunities for teachers to learn about their students' thinking and organize instruction around students' understandings. Researchers from the Children's Measurement project also use the *5 Practices* to directly connect LTs and the practices of teaching.

Learning trajectory based instruction involves bringing together research on student thinking and research on high-quality mathematics teaching, and the preceding chapters suggest that PD involving LTs should include opportunities for teachers to foster connections among LTs, mathematical tasks, and the practice of teaching. These connections can offer teachers ways to take up and use the knowledge represented in frameworks of student thinking in practice. For teachers, including tasks and frameworks for instructional practice in PD creates opportunities to envision how they might use student thinking to accomplish their goals for student learning. Likewise, the structure and details about student thinking included in LTs provide teachers with specific examples of learning that can support their implementation of recommendations about the use of tasks and the implementation of ambitious mathematics teaching. Therefore, we contend that connections between LTs and structures that support ambitious instruction, such as tasks and frameworks for instructional practices, are mutually beneficial and strengthen PD organized around LTs. When PD designers support teachers in establishing links between LTs and teaching, they help the development of a vision of teaching that can support the use of LTs to promote student learning in practice.

USING LTs TO FOSTER EQUITABLE TEACHING

Addressing inequities is the central issue of mathematics education of our time, and the relation between LTs and equitable teaching is perhaps the most important issue to consider when designing PD involving LTs. When ambitious instruction is equitable, one is unable to anticipate student participation and achievement in mathematics based on characteristics such as students' race, class, ethnicity, sex, or language proficiency (Gutiérrez, 2007). Instead, participation and achievement are considered in light of students' prior knowledge and experiences as well as evidence of their mathematical thinking.

Attending to students' mathematical thinking is a key practice of equitable mathematics teaching (Bartell, Wager, Edwards, Battey, Foote, & Spencer, 2017), and the preceding chapters offer numerous examples of how LTs provide teachers with a framework for recognizing and understanding student thinking. The LTBI project discusses how teachers began to recognize students' experiences outside of school as resources for learning. The Children's Measurement project describes that, as teachers further attended to student thinking, they realized they had underestimated students and adjusted their instruction in response. RTEM researchers discuss how teachers in their PD reported posing more questions, listening more, and developing a new respect for and focus on students' thinking. TRIAD researchers reported results of several studies showing that the implementation of their LT-based curriculum can lead to more equitable learning opportunities and outcomes for young children. These examples show that LTs can assist teachers in focusing on what students are thinking mathematically, instead of their race, class, sex, ethnicity, or language. This focus on student mathematical thinking can support more equitable teaching as teachers learn to make instructional decisions based on evidence of learning rather than on biases.

Nonetheless, using LTs in instruction does not always lead to more equitable opportunities and outcomes for students. Although all chapters discuss ways that LTs can support more equitable teaching, our experiences in the LTBI project show that LTs can be used to reproduce inequities. Thus, we add a word of caution in this chapter. For some teachers, rather than using LTs to focus on what students know as resources for learning, LTs can provide a way to express what students do not know and explain why students are not learning. Our experiences suggest that what teachers learn and how they use LTs is shaped by their perspectives on students, mathematics, teaching, and learning. For teachers with a strengths-based perspective, LTs provide guidance on how a student could continue learning based on what they know— and different chapters in this book discuss the importance of promoting a strengths-based perspective in PD involving LTs. However, as discussed in Chapter 2, LTs alone are insufficient to challenge deficit framings and may, in fact, reinforce them (Myers, 2014).

Perceptions of student ability can influence teachers' uses of LTs and, sometimes, LTs can also influence teachers' perceptions of ability. The Children's Measurement project reports that as teachers used LTs to plan and formatively assess student learning, they began to question previously held beliefs about their students' abilities and adjusted their instruction to include more sophisticated ways of thinking. On the other hand, LTBI researchers added more explicit attention to issues of equity in their PD design by establishing normative ways of discussing students' performance in mathematics. In particular, the project worked with teachers to examine their perceptions of students' mathematical abilities, which was a customary way of discussing students and their learning within the teachers' school and district. The added attention to equity supported teachers in attending to students' mathematical understanding and moving away from the discourse of "low and high" students they brought into the PD.

The strong influence of school and district discourses on these teachers' uses of LTs is a reminder that, in addition to teachers' existing knowledge, beliefs, and perceptions influencing their learning in PD, the norms and priorities of the schools and districts where teachers work have a profound impact on what they learn and how they use their learning in practice. Whereas teachers' prior knowledge and experiences are a regular consideration when designing PD, attending to teachers' contexts beyond the PD setting in meaningful ways is challenging. TRIAD researchers discussed a model of PD created to implement their LT-based curriculum for entire school districts, and their 10 guidelines highlight various points of contact between formal PD activities and teachers' school and district contexts and offer strategies for coordinating stakeholders and resources to support teachers.

To promote equitable teaching with LTs, we encourage PD designers to consider factors that mediate teachers' learning and use of LTs in practice. Decisions regarding the activities and tools included in PD are opportunities for PD designers to address teachers' prior knowledge and identities as well as their teaching context. In addition, designers might also consider addressing other components of equitable teaching in PD involving LTs. Including students' funds of knowledge as a part of an LT representation, developing an instructional framework for assigning competence, and adding a category about positioning students to frameworks for leading discussion are all examples of ways designers can promote the use of LTs and equitable teaching. What seems most important is to explicitly and purposefully consider a vision for equitable teaching when designing PDs that involve LTs and use this vision to promote discussions with teachers about beliefs, knowledge, and contexts.

CLOSING THOUGHTS

The benefits and potentials of using LTs in instruction and the importance of design for PD involving LTs are key contributions of the chapters in this book. Together, the projects address how teachers can learn about student thinking and ways to design PD around frameworks of student thinking to promote such learning. The three issues that are highlighted in this chapter—representing LTs for teachers, connecting LTs and teaching, and using LTs to foster equitable instruction—are important design considerations for PD involving frameworks of student thinking. The examples included suggest different and productive ways in which projects can engage with these issues in their PD design.

Learning about LTs can have several benefits for teachers, and the chapters in this book highlight how LTs and other frameworks of student thinking can promote teacher learning. Teachers come to use LTs in practice and make their teaching more attuned to students. LTs help teachers organize their teaching and, when used from a strengths-based perspective, support the implementation of more ambitious mathematics instruction. Thus, we suggest that LTs have the potential to transform mathematics teaching in ways that further align with current visions for what constitute high-quality instruction.

Equally important, the projects in this book demonstrate that careful attention to PD design is needed to promote teacher learning. Each project clearly had a set of design principles that made their PD effective. Each project was also responsive to teacher learning and worked to address teachers' needs in their design and in their practice of providing PD involving LTs. Combined, the projects demonstrate that carefully designing the ways in which the LTs are represented—connected to the actual practice of teaching, and used to promote equitable instruction—makes it possible for the PD to be designed to support teachers' use of frameworks of student thinking in teaching to achieve their ambitious goals for each and every student.

REFERENCES

Bartell, T., Wager, A., Edwards, A., Battey, D., Foote, M., & Spencer, J. (2017). Toward a framework for research linking equitable teaching with the standards for mathematical practice. *Journal for Research in Mathematics Education, 48*(1), 7–21.

Gutiérrez, R. (2007). (Re)defining equity: The importance of a civil perspective. In N. S. Nasir & P. Cobb (Eds.), *Improving access to mathematics: diversity and equity in the classroom.* New York, NY: Teachers College Press.

Myers, M. (2014). *The use of Learning Trajectory Based Instruction in supporting equitable teaching practices in elementary classrooms: A multi-case study* (Unpublished doctoral dissertation). North Carolina State University, Raleigh, NC.

Smith, M. S., & Stein, M. K. (2011). *5 practices for orchestrating productive mathematics discussions.* Reston, VA: National Council of Teachers of Mathematics.

Sztajn, P. (2011). Standards for reporting mathematics professional development in research studies. *Journal for Research in Mathematics Education, 42*(3), 220–236.

CHAPTER 7

Learning Trajectories in Mathematics Professional Development

A Commentary

Hilda Borko

When Holt and Paola invited me to write a short commentary chapter that situates the four projects presented here within the broader perspective of mathematics PD, the first thing I did (after reading the draft chapters) was to reread "Research on Mathematics Professional Development" (Sztajn, Borko & Smith, 2017), the chapter that Paola, Tom Smith, and I had recently written for the *Compendium for Research in Mathematics Education* (Cai, 2017). In that chapter we reviewed recent and emerging findings from research on mathematics PD using the three phases of research on professional development I had outlined almost 15 years ago (Borko, 2004). Phase 1 research examines PD programs offered at a single site to consider the potential effectiveness of the program; Phase 2 focuses on a single program enacted by more than one facilitator at more than one site and begins to explore the feasibility of scaling up the program; Phase 3 studies examine multiple PD programs to provide comparative information about resource requirements and effectiveness.

Interestingly, after reading the chapters describing the four projects in this book, I realized that these three research phases are not particularly helpful as a framework for analyzing the projects or situating them in the PD landscape. Technology-enhanced, Research-based, Instruction, Assessment, and professional Development (TRIAD, Chapter 5), with its scale-up study, fits the description of a Phase 2 project; however, the other three projects do not fit neatly into any of the phases (a point I return to later in the chapter). The two that most closely resemble Phase 1—the Learning Trajectories Based Instruction Project (LTBI, Chapter 2) and Children's Measurement Project (Chapter 3)—are much more extensive than programs typically studied in Phase 1 research. The research teams in those projects used a design-based research approach to develop and refine the PD programs, and they tracked changes in both the PD and teachers' learning across multiple iterations of the program. The Responsive Teaching in Elementary Mathematics project (RTEM, Chapter 4) also involved multiple cycles of development and research. In addition, it used multiple facilitators to conduct the PD at multiple sites. However, unlike Phase 2 research, in this chapter the research team did not compare implementation or findings across sites, and they did not address questions about scale.

In contrast to the phases of research, several of the themes Paola, Tom, and I used to organize research within each phase, and the issues we identified as important areas for additional research, proved more useful for considering the contributions of these projects to the literature. In this chapter, I consider the projects with respect to several of these issues: the role of different types of tools in mathematics professional development; approaches to bringing PD programs to scale, including the role of technological tools; and design-based research as a promising research methodology.

THE ROLE OF TOOLS IN
MATHEMATICS PROFESSIONAL DEVELOPMENT

Phase 1 studies represented almost 75% of the papers reviewed for the *Compendium* chapter. Most of the studies in this phase incorporated five consensus features of effective PD (e.g., Desimone, 2009): a focus on subject matter content, teachers' active learning, collective participation, coherence, and adequate duration, thus adding support to Desimone's claim that there is consensus regarding the role of these features in effective PD. These features, however, seem to be necessary but not sufficient to effect change. Several studies offer evidence that PD programs designed with these features can produce significant gains in teacher knowledge and instructional practices (e.g., Bell, Wilson, Higgins, & McCoach, 2010) and student learning (e.g., Kiemer, Groschner, Pehmer, & Seidel, 2015; Penuel, Gallagher, & Moorthy, 2011). Other studies, however, show that simply including the five features of effective PD is insufficient to ensure positive impacts for teachers or students (Garet et al., 2008; Garet et al., 2011).

One reason the consensus features are insufficient is that they are not specific enough to guide PD design decisions. Wayne, Yoon, Zhu, Cronen and Garet (2008) and Wilson (2013) identified several areas in which additional research is needed, including identification of the mechanisms underlying teacher learning and more detailed specification of PD practices and resources.

We organized the discussion of Phase 1 research in the *Compendium* chapter around tools, which enabled us to focus on design elements beyond the consensus features and to examine PD practices and resources. Three types of tools were prominent in the PD programs we reviewed: frameworks of student mathematical thinking, video clips of mathematics instruction, and mathematical tasks. Similarly, the four PD programs featured in this book used a variety of tools to achieve their goals for teacher learning. In what follows, I compare tool use across the programs to offer additional insights about the role of tools in mathematics PD. I first briefly review the relevant findings and conclusions in Sztajn, Borko and Smith (2017), focusing primarily on frameworks of student mathematical thinking because that is the tool most closely aligned with LTs. Next, I suggest another framework for analyzing the role of pedagogical tools in teaching and teacher learning. I then use this framework to situate the LT projects in the PD literature.

Tools Used in Phase 1 Mathematics Professional Development Programs

An important design feature of the Phase 1 PD programs we reviewed was its use of tools such as frameworks of student thinking, video clips, and mathematical tasks to ground the PD in an aspect of teachers' practice. We found, for example, that PD organized around frameworks of student mathematical thinking supported teachers in learning to elicit and interpret student thinking, and to build on students' ideas during instruction. We also learned that tools such as frameworks, video clips, and mathematical tasks are often used in combination in PD programs. We concluded that "more research is needed to examine how different tools come together in the design of PD experiences to foster (or hinder) teacher learning in mathematics PD programs" (p. 801). Our conclusion did not suggest differentiated roles for different types of tools. When considering how to situate the four LT projects within this literature, however, I wondered whether learning trajectories play a different role in the design and enactment of PD experiences than tools such as video, mathematical tasks, and student work. This wondering led me to the scholarship of Pam Grossman and colleagues, who examined the role of pedagogical tools in the process of learning to teach English.

Conceptual and Practical Pedagogical Tools

In their research project focused on novice teachers' process of learning to teach English, Pam Grossman and colleagues (Grossman, Smagorinsky, & Valencia, 1999; Grossman et al., 2000) examined the tools that teachers use to plan and enact classroom practice. They drew from activity theory (Wertsch, 1981, 1985) to make a distinction between two types of pedagogical tools: conceptual tools and practical tools. *Conceptual tools* are "principles, frameworks, and ideas about teaching [and] learning . . . that teachers use as heuristics to guide decisions about teaching and learning" (Grossman et al., 1999, p. 14), and to ensure that their goals, curriculum, instruction, and assessment are aligned. *Practical tools*, on the other hand, are classroom practices, strategies, and resources such as daily and unit plans, textbooks, and instructional materials. These tools "do not serve as broad conceptions to guide an array of decisions but, instead, have more local and immediate utility" (p. 14).

On the basis of their analysis of preservice teachers' transitions into teaching, Grossman and colleagues (2000) suggested that although conceptual tools are useful for a broad understanding of teaching and learning, "they do not solve the problem of what to do in the classroom" (p. 634). Practical tools are the concrete strategies and resources that can be used to address this problem. Without an adequate repertoire of practical tools, some novice English teachers in their study encountered difficulties trying to teach in ways that were compatible with the conceptual tools such as instructional scaffolding and process writing that they appropriated from their university courses. Conversely, when practical tools were not grounded in concepts, some teachers found it difficult to evaluate new strategies or envision alternatives. The research team concluded that conceptual and practical tools are both necessary for teachers to successfully enact new visions of teaching and learning.

Using Grossman and colleagues' definitions, LTs are conceptual tools whereas mathematical tasks, video clips, and student work are practical tools. This categorization suggests that LTs can be used to guide a variety of decisions in designing PD, while tasks, student work, and video clips have immediate utility for enacting specific PD activities. In the next section, I consider whether an analysis of the roles that the two types of tools play in the four LT programs would bear out this distinction, and whether the analysis might contribute to our understanding of how different types of tools are combined in the design and enactment of PD experiences. More specifically, I conjecture that LTs might be used to guide decisions about what practical tools to use, as well as how and when to use them—decisions that, as we suggested, are in need of further research (Sztajn, Borko, & Smith, 2017). For example, an LT focused on geometric shapes might guide decisions about the order in which to present different sets of student work for teachers to analyze. An LT focused on fractions might guide the PD designer to select video clips depicting students struggling with specific types of problems during small-group discussions. To test this idea, I review the roles that tools play in each PD project and then consider similarities and differences in tool use across the projects. It is important to note that in all four projects, LTs had two distinct, yet compatible, roles—both as a central focus of the PD and as a tool for guiding PD design. I primarily address the role of LTs in designing the PD programs.

Learning Trajectories and Other Pedagogical Tools

How can the use of pedagogical tools in the four PD programs contribute to our understanding of ways in which combinations of tools might foster teacher learning? All four PD programs use a combination of conceptual and practical tools. In what follows, I examine some of the ways in which they do so. I then discuss how their approaches support the design of PD programs.

The Learning Trajectories Based Instruction (LTBI) created several *professional learning tasks* that use a variety of practical tools—artifacts of practice—to situate teachers' learning in the practice of teaching (Ball & Cohen, 1999). The summer institute focused on using LTs to examine and understand students' mathematical thinking. Professional learning tasks typically entailed using LTs to analyze student work and to watch and discuss video clips of instruction, and LTs guided both the development and selection of artifacts and the use of the artifacts in the PD activities. During the school year, the LTs also served as a conceptual tool that guided the selection and use of the practical tools (mathematics tasks).

In the Children's Measurement Project, the research team explained, "Using an LT in instruction involves separate yet related tasks of teaching (i.e., developing tasks, identifying important aspects of students' work, interpreting students' understanding" [Barrett et al., this volume]). The PD activities incorporate several practical tools to address these tasks of teaching, including mathematical tasks, videos of students solving the tasks, and examples of student work. The research team designed the PD to support teachers in using the LTs as a framework for analyzing students' thinking and reasoning about measurement topics in the videos and samples of student work, and as a guide for modifying classroom tasks or developing new measurement tasks to fit their mathematical goals. In addition, they used the LTs to guide development of the PD activities. They also used a second conceptual tool, the *teacher-noticing framework* (Jacobs, Lamb, & Philipp, 2010), in designing these activities. Thus, similarly to their role in LTBI, LTs guided both the researchers' selection and organization of practical tools in PD activities, and teachers' analysis of students' mathematical understanding depicted in the practical tools.

The Responsive Teaching in Elementary Mathematics (RTEM) professional development introduces teachers to four conceptual tools—two frameworks of student thinking (the *problem-type framework* and *strategy framework*) and two frameworks of instructional practices (the *noticing framework* and *questioning framework*). It engages teachers in a variety of activities designed to support their responsiveness by helping them use the frameworks to make student thinking visible, and to organize and use what they see and hear when students are solving problems. Practical tools also play a central role in the PD activities, which include, for example, solving mathematics problems using children's strategies; analyzing children's written work; watching videos of individual children solving problems; and reviewing and adapting curriculum materials through a lens of children's thinking. The frameworks of children's thinking guided selection of two sets of practical tools—the video and written-work artifacts—which were chosen to showcase specific aspects of children's thinking. The research team commented that selection of the practical tools was particularly challenging, as the activities in which they are used must systematically introduce teachers to, and give them practice with, both frameworks of children's thinking and frameworks of instructional practices.

In _Building Blocks_ and TRIAD, LTs in two domains—numeric and quantitative, spatial and geometric—are central to both the curriculum and the PD program. The role of the LTs in TRIAD is similar to their role in the LTBI and Children's Measurement projects. That is, they are intended to be used by teachers to guide and support their mathematics instruction. However, TRIAD differs from the other three PD programs in that one of the practical tools—the set of instructional activities—is embedded in the LTs. Similar to the other programs, additional practical tools such as PD activities for the teachers and videos of best practices are based on the LTs. One key difference between TRIAD and the other PD projects featured in this book is the centrality of a technological tool. The Learning and Teaching with Learning Trajectories (LT2) web application provides access to resources that comprise the TRIAD PD—both descriptions of the LTs and concrete tools such as the _Building Blocks_ instructional activities; PD activities for teachers; and videos of best practices. As a technological tool, LT2 differs from both conceptual and practical pedagogical tools.

Given that this book "focuses on understanding how teachers can learn to make LTs central to their teaching" (Sztajn & Wilson, this volume), it is not surprising that all four programs feature LTs as one, if not the only, conceptual tool. In all four, LTs are used to design learning experiences for children. The same LTs (or frameworks of student thinking) play multiple roles in the PD programs. In addition to having teachers' understanding and use of the LTs in their practice as a central goal, all four projects used these conceptual tools to design and organize the PD experiences. The LTBI design team created _professional learning tasks_ to support teachers' learning of the LTs. The Children's Measurement Project and TRIAD also included specific PD activities designed to support teachers' learning of the LTs. In the RTEM project, the PD engages teachers in a variety of activities in which they use the frameworks of children's thinking to analyze children's mathematical understanding and problem-solving strategies, and to review and adapt curriculum materials.

PD activities in the four programs also draw upon practical tools— artifacts such as student work and video clips from classroom lessons—to situate teachers' learning in the practice of teaching. In each case, LTs guided the selection, creation, and organization of these practical tools. The Children's Measurement Project and RTEM used the LTs in combination with conceptual tools focused on instructional practices. In both projects, these conceptual tools were used together to guide the development and use of the practical tools. Thus, in all four PD programs conceptual and practical tools played different, and complementary, roles. Whereas conceptual tools guided the development and use of practical tools, the practical tools were central to teachers learning to use the conceptual tools in their teaching. This combination of conceptual and practical tools, therefore, seems key to design of these PD programs. Further, as more PD programs incorporate technological tools such as LT2, it will be interesting to see if these tools influence the use of conceptual and practical tools in PD and the relationships between them.

LEARNING TRAJECTORIES AND BRINGING PROFESSIONAL DEVELOPMENT TO SCALE

In our review of Phase 2 research, Paola, Tom, and I identified two approaches used to bring PD to multiple sites: developing a PD curriculum and materials for facilitators; and working with education agencies at the district, state, or national level to build local capacity to conduct PD. I focus primarily on the first approach since none of the chapters in this book describes project work with education agencies to build PD capacity.

The chapter on the TRIAD project was the only one that discussed scalability and sustainability and was more in line with Phase 2. The TRIAD PD is, in some sense, a professional development curriculum in that it consists of sessions to address the LTs for each mathematics topic. Each session includes experiences and resources to support teachers' learning of the three components of LTs: goals, developmental progressions, and activities. The TRIAD team describes the PD as adaptive and the experiences and resources are provided through the Learning and Teaching with Learning Trajectories (LT2) web-based technological tool. In the next sections, I explore how these two features of TRIAD contribute to our understanding of approaches to bringing PD to scale.

Adaptivity and Specificity

Koellner and Seago (2010) proposed that PD models can be located on a continuum from highly adaptive to highly specified. As they explained, highly adaptive models are designed to be responsive to a local context, whereas in highly specified models the goals, content, and facilitation materials, often available in published form, are designed to ensure a predetermined PD experience. Building on this work, Koellner and Jacobs (2015) suggested that the construct of adaptability has important implications for how PD research is conducted and how research findings are interpreted. Because adaptive models are continually evolving, in comparison to highly specified models, it is more difficult to study their impact or to predict whether the program's impact at a particular time will be a valid indicator of impact for future iterations of the program.

As we noted in the *Compendium* chapter, projects that developed PD curricula and materials for facilitators have provided initial evidence that highly specified PD models can be effective tools for scaling up professional development. For example, research on the Developing Mathematical Ideas (DMI; Bell, Wilson, Higgins, & McCoach, 2010) and Learning and Teaching Geometry (LTG; Seago et al., 2017) programs demonstrated that highly specified PD curricula can be implemented at multiple sites with fidelity to their key features, as well as evidence that they can result in gains in teacher and student learning.

Koellner and Jacobs provided evidence from Implementing the Problem-Solving Cycle (iPSC)—a Phase 2 research project to investigate the scalability, sustainability, and impact of the Problem-Solving Cycle (PSC) professional development model—that adaptive PD programs can also be scaled up effectively. The research team prepared local PD leaders to implement the PSC. Participants in the PSC workshops they led showed modest improvements in mathematical knowledge for teaching and classroom instruction. This project thus adds to the field's understanding of building local capacity as an approach to bringing PD to multiple sites. However, because the PSC is not a PD curriculum, it does not address questions about the scalability of adaptive PD curricula.

Research on the TRIAD program does address that question. At first glance, I placed TRIAD toward the highly specified end of the adaptability continuum. In fact, of the four LT-based PD programs, RTEM seems like the only one that is highly adaptive, whereas the others fall more toward the highly specified end of the continuum. A closer examination of the four programs, however, suggests that a more nuanced approach to adaptability and its potential role in scaling up PD is warranted. Focusing specifically on TRIAD, detailed research-based LTs are at the core of TRIAD PD. The PD sessions address LTs for each mathematics topic and include goals and activities for children at each developmental level. However, as Sarama and Clements pointed out, program guidelines emphasize to "give latitude for adaptation to teachers and schools but maintain integrity," and to "help teachers distinguish productive adaptations from lethal mutations" (this volume).

The TRIAD program demonstrates that a PD curriculum can have adaptive as well as specified components. This characteristic suggests that rather than a continuum of adaptability, it may be more useful to conceive of adaptability as multidimensional and to carefully consider what elements of a PD program are meant to be adaptive and what elements are specified, both when enacting the PD and when designing research to study its impact. This conception of adaptability also suggests that PD designers should be explicit about which elements of PD are intended to be adaptive and provide guidelines for adapting those elements to particular teachers, students, and contexts.

The Role of Technology in Bringing Professional Development to Scale

Our review of mathematics PD research in the *Compendium* chapter pointed out that online and blended PD opportunities are becoming more prevalent and are being advertised as a way to bring PD to scale. However, our literature search turned up very few studies of online or hybrid PD programs in mathematics. We suggested that the use of technology as a mode of interaction in PD is an important area for future research (Sztajn, Borko, & Smith, 2017). The TRIAD project contributes to this emerging area of research. The TRIAD PD was designed to support teachers' learning and implementation of the LTs introduced in the *Building Blocks* curriculum. The PD sessions, developed by the research team, are made available through the LT2 technological tool. The research team attributed success of the TRIAD program, at least in part, to the coherence of their model of professional development, curriculum, instruction, and assessment based on the LTs. The fact that the PD model, including the three components of the LTs (goals, developmental progressions, and instructional activities) was made available through the LT2 technological tool undoubtedly contributed to the feasibility of conducting such a large scale-up study. LT2 also gave teachers access to the *Building Blocks* curriculum and LTs after their participation in the intervention. These two features of the project, coupled with results of the scale-up study, attest to the valuable role that online platforms can play in making high-quality mathematics PD available to all teachers on an ongoing basis.

DESIGN-BASED RESEARCH AS AN APPROACH TO DEVELOPING AND STUDYING PROFESSIONAL DEVELOPMENT

In addition to their substantive contributions to our understanding of teacher learning, the projects featured in this book provide methodological contributions to the design and study of professional development. The TRIAD project is the only one that fits neatly into the framework of three research phases we used to organize our review of mathematics PD research in the *Compendium*. The other three projects are more extensive in scope than typical Phase 1 research; yet, they do not address Phase 2 questions related to sustainability and scale. In this section, I explore one way in which these three projects extend the three-phase framework and the methodological contributions of their approach.

When presenting the three-phase framework (Borko, 2004), I acknowledged that the three phases represent only "one way in which research activities can progress toward the goal of providing high-quality professional development for all teachers" (p. 4). I also cautioned that "A professional development program must be well defined and clearly specified before researchers can investigate how it is enacted by multiple facilitators in multiple settings, and what resources are needed to ensure its effectiveness" (p. 9), questions that are at the core of Phase 2 research. Phase 1 research is designed to provide an existence proof—evidence that a professional development program can have a positive impact on teacher learning. Reflecting on this caution, it seems clear that not all PD programs shown to be effective in Phase 1 studies are ready for Phase 2 investigations. The multiyear projects to develop the LTBI, Children's Measurement Project, and RTEM demonstrate one set of intermediary steps between Phase 1 and Phase 2 research. They also attest to the value of these steps.

In the review of mathematics PD research (Sztajn, Borko, & Smith, 2017), we suggested that design-based implementation research (DBIR; Fishman, Penuel, Allen, Cheng, & Sabelli, 2013; Penuel, Fishman, Cheng, & Sabelli, 2011), with its dual focus on building theory and developing capacity for sustainable change in systems, offers a promising approach to Phase 2 research. Design-based research is similar to DBIR, but without the focus on institutional change or working with multiple levels of an educational system (Cobb, Confrey, diSessa, Lehrer, & Schauble, 2003; Design-Based Research Collective, 2003). In classroom-based design research, for example, the research team works collaboratively with teachers to improve practice, and it contributes to theory by creating models of successful educational innovations and developing explanatory frameworks about both the processes of learning and the tools to foster learning (e.g., Cobb, 1999; Cobb, McClain, & Gravemeijer, 2003).

LTBI, Children's Measurement Project, and RTEM all used a design-based research approach to develop and refine their PD models. For example, the Children's Measurement Project conducted six rounds of PD. Participating teachers were invited to contribute recommendations for simplifying the descriptions of LT levels and, as Jeffrey Barrett and colleagues reported, "successive cycles produced less complex, more focused accounts of children's learning about measures of length, area, and volume" (this volume). Similar to design-based classroom research, the three projects also "provide a lens for understanding how theoretical claims about teaching and learning can be transformed into effective learning in educational settings" (Design-Based Research Collective, 2003, p. 8). In these projects, the PD programs were central to transforming the theoretical claims—the LTs—into effective classroom teaching and learning activities. Focusing on another educational setting, the research teams also transformed the LTs into effective PD learning activities. The teams' experiences, and the PD models they developed, suggest that design-based research, with its iterative cycles of design, implementation, analysis, and revisions, is an effective way to refine and clearly specify a PD model shown to be effective in a Phase 1 study so that it is ready to be used by multiple facilitators and studied in Phase 2 research.

CONCLUDING THOUGHTS

Chapters 2 through 5 include much more information about the process of designing a professional development program than is typically available to readers. As I hope this commentary illustrates, the depth of description here provides valuable insights for both PD designers and researchers. The projects highlight the importance of incorporating conceptual and practical tools into the design of PD experiences, and they suggest ways that each type of tool can inform use of the other tool. They illustrate that a PD program can have both adaptive and specified components and demonstrate the importance of guidelines for developing adaptations that are productive and that maintain integrity with the program's underlying principles. Several projects also underscore the value of having teachers actively participate in the design of PD programs, and they illustrate different ways in which teachers can be involved in the design process. In addition, they emphasize the value of design-based research for both designing effective PD programs and studying their effectiveness.

REFERENCES

Ball, D. L., & Cohen, D. K. (1999). Developing practice, developing practitioners: Toward a practice-based theory of professional education. In L. Darling-Hammond & G. Sykes (Eds.), *Teaching as the learning profession: Handbook of policy and practice* (pp. 3–32). San Francisco, CA: Jossey-Bass.

Bell, C. A., Wilson, S. M., Higgins, T., & McCoach, D. B. (2010). Measuring the effects of professional development on teacher knowledge: The case of developing mathematical ideas. *Journal for Research in Mathematics Education, 41*(5), 479–512.

Borko, H. (2004). Professional development and teacher learning: Mapping the terrain. *Educational Researcher, 33,* 3–15.

Cai, J. (Ed.). (2017). *Compendium for research in mathematics education.* Reston, VA: National Council of Teachers of Mathematics.

Cobb, P. (1999). Individual and collective mathematical development: The case of statistical data analysis. *Mathematical Thinking and Learning, 1*(1), 5–44.

Cobb, P., Confrey, J., diSessa, A., Lehrer, R., & Schauble, L. (2003). Design experiments in education research. *Educational Researcher, 32*(1), 9–13.

Cobb, P., McClain, K., & Gravemeijer, K. P. E. (2003). Learning about statistical covariation. *Cognition and Instruction, 21*(1), 1–78.

Design-Based Research Collective (2003). Design-based research: An emerging paradigm for educational inquiry. *Educational Researcher, 32*(1), 5–8.

Desimone, L. M. (2009). Improving impact studies of teachers' professional development: Toward better conceptualizations and measures. *Educational Researcher*, *38*(3), 181–199.

Fishman, B. J., Penuel, W. R., Allen, A.-R., Cheng, B. H., & Sabelli, N. (2013). Design-based implementation research: An emerging model for transforming the relationship of research and practice. In B. J. Fishman, W. R. Penuel, A. Allen, & B. H. Cheng (Eds.), *Design-based implementation research: Theories, methods, and exemplars*. National Society for the Study of Education Yearbook (Vol. 112, pp. 136–156). New York, NY: Teachers College Record.

Garet, M. S., Cronen, S., Eaton, M., Kurki, A., Ludwig, M., Jones, W., . . . Silverberg, M. (2008). *The impact of two professional development interventions on early reading instruction and achievement*. Washington, DC: National Center for Education Evaluation and Regional Assistance.

Garet, M. S., Wayne, A. J., Stancavage, F., Taylor, J., Eaton, M., Walters, K., . . . Hurlburt, S. (2011). *Middle school mathematics professional development impact study: Findings after the second year of implementation* (No. NCEE 2011-4024). Washington, DC: National Center for Education Evaluation and Regional Assistance.

Grossman, P. L., Smagorinsky, P., & Valencia, S. (1999). Appropriating tools for teaching English: A theoretical framework for research on learning to teach. *American Journal of Education*. *108*, 1–29.

Grossman, P. L., Valencia, S., Evans, K., Thompson, C., Martin, S., & Place, N. (2000). Transitions into teaching: Learning to teach writing in teacher education and beyond. *Journal of Literacy Research, 32*, 631–662.

Jacobs, V. R., Lamb, C. E., & Philipp, R. A. (2010). Professional noticing of children's mathematical thinking. *Journal for Research in Mathematics Education, 41*(2), 169–202.

Kiemer, K., Groschner, A., Pehmer, A., & Seidel, T. (2015). Effects of a classroom discourse intervention on teachers' practice and students' motivation to learn mathematics and science. *Learning and Instruction, 35*, 94.

Koellner, K., & Jacobs, J. (2015). Distinguishing models of professional development: The case of an adaptive model's impact on teachers' knowledge, instruction, and student achievement. *Journal of Teacher Education, 66*(1), 51–67.

Koellner, K., & Seago, N. (2010). Using video to study teacher learning: The role of the facilitator. In M. Pinto & T. F. Kawasaki (Eds.), *Proceedings of the 34th Conference of the International Group for the Psychology of Mathematics Education, Vol.1* (p. 392). Belo Horizonte, Brazil.

Penuel, W. R., Fishman, B. J., Cheng, B. H., & Sabelli, N. (2011). Organizing research and development at the intersection of learning, implementation, and design. *Educational Researcher, 40*(7), 331–337.

Penuel, W. R., Gallagher, L. P., & Moorthy, S. (2011). Preparing teachers to design sequences of instruction in earth systems science: A comparison of three professional development programs. *American Educational Research Journal, 48*(4), 996–1025.

Seago, N., Jacobs, J., Driscoll, M., Callahan, P., Matassa, M., & Nikula, J. (2017). *Learning and teaching geometry: Video cases for mathematics professional development, grades 5–10*. San Francisco, CA: WestEd.

Sztajn, P., Borko, H., & Smith, T. S. (2017). Research on mathematics professional development. In Cai, J. (Ed.), *Compendium for research in mathematics education* (pp. 213–243). Reston, VA: National Council of Teachers of Mathematics.

Wayne, A. J., Yoon, K. S., Zhu, P., Cronen, S., & Garet, M. S. (2008). Experimenting with teacher professional development: Motives and methods. *Educational Researcher, 37*(8), 469.

Wertsch, J. V. (1981). The concept of activity in Soviet psychology: An introduction. In J. V. Wertsch (Ed.), *The concept of activity in Soviet psychology* (pp. 3–36),. Armonk, NY: Sharpe.

Wertsch, J. V. (1985). Vygotsky and the social formation of mind. Cambridge, MA: Harvard University Press.

Wilson, S. M. (2013). Professional development for science teachers. *Science, 340*(6130), 310–313.

About the Contributors

Jae M. Baek is a mathematics educator at Illinois State University. She studies how children make sense of mathematical concepts and how teachers support children's thinking.

Jeffrey E. Barrett is a professor of mathematics education at Illinois State University. He studies children's growing knowledge of the intersection of space and number and how to teach geometric measurement.

Hilda Borko is a professor of education at Stanford University. Her research explores teacher cognition and instructional practices, the process of learning to teach, the impact of teacher professional development programs on teachers and students, the preparation of PD leaders, and educational research-practice partnerships.

Douglas H. Clements is Distinguished University Professor, Kennedy Endowed Chair in Early Childhood Learning, and executive director of the Marsico Institute at the University of Denver. His research focuses on learning and teaching of early mathematics using learning trajectories and computer applications in mathematics education.

Amanda L. Cullen is an assistant professor in the Mathematics Department at Illinois State University. Her research focuses on teachers' use of hypothetical learning trajectories as instructional tools and elementary and middle school students' development of geometric measurement concepts.

Craig J. Cullen is an associate professor of mathematics education at Illinois State University. His research interests include students' development of an understanding of measurement and the use of technology in the teaching and learning of mathematics.

Cyndi Edgington is an assistant teaching professor of mathematics education at North Carolina State University. Her teaching and research focus on student-centered mathematics instruction.

Susan B. Empson holds the Richard G. Miller endowed chair in mathematics education at the University of Missouri. Her research focuses on children's mathematical thinking and teachers' development in elementary schools.

Amy Hewitt is a doctoral student of mathematics education at the University of North Carolina at Greensboro. Her research focuses on selecting and sequencing student work for whole-class discussions in elementary mathematics classrooms.

Victoria R. Jacobs is the Yopp Distinguished Professor of Mathematics Education at the University of North Carolina at Greensboro. Her research involves long-term collaborations with teachers to explore children's mathematical thinking and how that thinking can inform instruction.

Naomi Jessup is an assistant professor of mathematics education at Georgia State University. Her research focuses on mathematics teacher learning, children's mathematical thinking, teacher noticing, and framing.

Gladys Krause is an assistant professor of mathematics education at William and Mary College. Her research centers on teacher knowledge and children's mathematical thinking, and how these two areas interact in classroom settings that involve multilingual and multicultural dynamics.

Marrielle Myers is an assistant professor of elementary mathematics education at Kennesaw State University. Her research focuses on preparing preservice teachers to use mathematics as a tool for social justice and supporting preservice teachers of color in navigating field experiences.

D'Anna Pynes is a postdoctoral research fellow at the University of Michigan–Ann Arbor. Her research focuses on mathematics teacher learning, professional development settings, and teacher communities.

Julie Sarama is the Kennedy Endowed Chair in Innovative Learning Technologies and Distinguished University Professor at the University of Denver. She conducts research on young children's development of mathematical concepts and competencies, implementation and scale-up of educational reform, professional development models and their influence on student learning, and implementation and effects of software environments (including those she has created) in mathematics classrooms.

Paola Sztajn is a professor of mathematics education and associate dean for research and innovation at North Carolina State University. Her research focuses on elementary teachers' professional development and knowledge in mathematics.

Jennifer M. Tobias is an associate professor of mathematics education at Illinois State University. Her research interests include the development of prospective elementary teachers' understanding of rational number concepts and operations and the professional development of teachers.

Jared Webb is an assistant professor of mathematics education at North Carolina A&T State University. His research focuses on prospective and practicing mathematics teacher learning and the design of mathematics learning environments.

Megan H. Wickstrom is an assistant professor of mathematics education at Montana State University in Bozeman, Montana. Her research focuses on exploring K–12 teachers' geometric content knowledge and finding ways to support them in developing rich, mathematical tasks that respond to students' emergent thinking.

P. Holt Wilson is an associate professor of mathematics education at the University of North Carolina at Greensboro. His research focuses on mathematics teacher learning and professional development design.

Index